AN E
THE GOS

MA

VOLUME 1
(CHAPTER 6:5-24)

THE
PREACHER'S
OUTLINE & SERMON
BIBLE®

NEW TESTAMENT

NEW INTERNATIONAL VERSION

LEADERSHIP MINISTRIES WORLDWIDE
P.O. Box 21310
Chattanooga, TN 37424

Publisher & Distributor

DEDICATED:

To all the men and women of the world
who preach and teach the Gospel of our
Lord Jesus Christ and
To the Mercy and Grace of God.

- Demonstrated to us in Christ Jesus our Lord.

  "In him we have redemption through his blood, the forgiveness
  of sins, in accordance with the riches of God's grace."

  (Eph. 1:7 NIV)

- Out of the mercy and grace of God His Word has
  flowed. Let every person know that God will have
  mercy upon him, forgiving and using him to fulfill
  His glorious plan of salvation.

  "For God so loved the world, that he gave his one and only
  Son, that whosoever believes in him shall not perish, but
  have eternal life. For God did not send his Son into the world
  to condemn the world, but to save the world through him."

  (Jn. 3:16-17 NIV)

  "This is good and pleases God our Saviour; who wants all
  men to be saved and to come to the knowledge of the truth."

  (1 Tim. 2:3-4 NIV)

The Preacher's Outline and Study Bible®–NIV
is written for God's servants to use in their
study, teaching, and preaching of God's Holy Word.

OUR VISION – PASSION – PURPOSE

- To share the Word of God with the world.
- To help the believer, both minister and layman alike, in
  his understanding, preaching, and teaching of God's
  Word.
- To do everything we possibly can to lead men, women,
  boys, and girls to give their hearts and lives to Jesus
  Christ and to secure the eternal life which He offers.
- To do all we can to minister to the needy of the world.
- To give Jesus Christ His proper place, the place which
  the Word gives Him. Therefore— No work of Leadership
  Ministries Worldwide will ever be personalized.

ACKNOWLEDGMENTS

Every child of God is precious to the Lord and deeply loved. And every child as a servant of the Lord touches the lives of those who come in contact with him or his ministry. The writing ministry of the following servants have touched this work, and we are grateful that God brought their writings our way. We hereby acknowledge their ministry to us, being fully aware that there are so many others down through the years whose writings have touched our lives and who deserve mention, but the weaknesses of our minds have caused them to fade from memory. May our wonderful Lord continue to bless the ministry of these dear servants, and the ministry of us all as we diligently labor to reach the world for Christ and to meet the desperate needs of those who suffer so much.

THE GREEK SOURCES

1. Expositor's Greek Testament, Edited by W. Robertson Nicoll. Grand Rapids, MI: Eerdmans Publishing Co., 1970
2. Robertson, A.T. Word Pictures in the New Testament. Nashville, TN: Broadman Press, 1930.
3. Thayer, Joseph Henry. Greek-English Lexicon of the New Testament. New York: American Book Co. No date listed.
4. Vincent, Marvin R. Word Studies in the New Testament. Grand Rapids, MI: Eerdmans Publishing Co., 1969
5. Vine, W.E. Expository Dictionary of New Testament Words. Old Tappan, NJ: Fleming H. Revell Co. No date listed.
6. Wuest, Kenneth S. Word Studies in the Greek New Testament. Grand Rapids, MI: Eerdmans Publishing Co., 1966.

THE REFERENCE WORKS

7. Cruden's Complete Concordance of the Old & New Testament. Philadelphia, PA: The John C. Winston Co., 1930.
8. Josephus' Complete Works. Grand Rapids, MI: Kregel Publications, 1981.
9. Lockyer, Herbert. Series of Books, including his Books on All the Men, Women, Miracles, and Parables of the Bible. Grand Rapids, MI: Zondervan Publishing House, 1958-1967.
10. -Nave's Topical Bible. Nashville, TN: The Southwestern Co., No date listed.

11. <u>The Amplified New Testament</u>. (Scripture Quotations are from the Amplified New Testament, Copyright 1954, 1958, 1987 by the Lockman Foundation. Used by permission.)

12. <u>The Four Translation New Testament</u> (Including King James, New American Standard, Williams–New Testament In the Language of the People, Beck - New Testament In the Language of Today.) Minneapolis, MN: World Wide Publications.

13. <u>The New Compact Bible Dictionary</u>, Edited by T. Alton Bryant. Grand Rapids, MI: Zondervan Publishing House, 1967.

14. <u>The New Thompson Chain Reference Bible</u>. Indianapolis, IN: B.B. Kirkbride Bible Co., 1964.

THE COMMENTARIES

15. Barclay, William. <u>Daily Study Bible Series</u>. Philadelphia, PA: Westminster Press, Began in 1953.

16. Bruce, F.F. <u>The Epistle to the Ephesians</u>. Westwood, NJ: Fleming H. Revell Co., 1968.

17. Bruce, F.F. <u>Epistle to the Hebrews</u>. Grand Rapids, MI: Eerdmans Publishing Co., 1964.

18. Bruce, F.F. <u>The Epistles of John</u>. Old Tappan, NJ: Fleming H. Revell Co., 1970.

19. Criswell, W.A. <u>Expository Sermons on Revelation</u>. Grand Rapids, MI: Zondervan Publishing House, 1962-66.

20. Greene, Oliver. <u>The Epistles of John</u>. Greenville, SC: The Gospel Hour, Inc., 1966.

21. Greene, Oliver. <u>The Epistles of Paul the Apostle to Timothy and Titus</u>. Greenville, SC: The Gospel Hour, Inc., 1965.

22. Greene, Oliver. <u>The Epistles of Paul the Apostle to Timothy and Titus</u>. Greenville, SC: The Gospel Hour, Inc. 1964.

23. Greene, Oliver. <u>The Revelation Verse by Verse Study</u>. Greenville, SC: The Gospel Hour, Inc., 1963.

24. Henry, Matthew. <u>Commentary on the Whole Bible</u>. Old Tappan, NJ: Fleming H. Revell Co.

25. Hodge, Charles. <u>Exposition on Romans & on Corinthians</u>. Grand Rapids, MI: Eerdmans Publishing Co., 1972-1973.

26. Ladd, George Eldon. <u>A Commentary On the Revelation of John</u>. Grand Rapids, MI: Eerdmans Publishing Co., 1972-1973.

27. Leupold, H.C. <u>Exposition of Daniel</u>. Grand Rapids, MI: Baker Book House, 1969.

28. Morris, Leon. <u>The Gospel According to John</u>. Grand Rapids, MI: Eerdmans Publishing Co., 1971.

29. Newell, William R. <u>Hebrews, Verse by Verse</u>. Chicago, IL: Moody Press, 1947.

30. Strauss, Lehman. <u>Devotional Studies in Galatians & Ephesians</u>. Neptune, NJ: Loizeaux Brothers, 1957.

31. Strauss, Lehman. <u>Devotional Studies in Philippians</u>. Neptune, NJ: Loizeaux Brothers, 1959.

32. Strauss, Lehman. <u>James, Your Brother</u>. Neptune, NJ: Loizeaux Brothers, 1956.

33. Strauss, Lehman. <u>The Book of the Revelation</u>. Neptune, NJ: Loizeaux Brothers, 1964.

34. <u>The New Testament & Wycliffe Bible Commentary</u>, Edited by Charles F. Pfeiffer & Everett F. Harrison. New York: The Iverson Associates, 1971. Produced for Moody Monthly. Chicago Moody Press, 1962.

35. <u>The Pulpit Commentary</u>, Edited by H.D.M. Spence & Joseph S. Exell. Grand Rapids, MI: Eerdmans Publishing Co., 1950.

36. Thomas, W.H. Griffith. <u>Hebrews, A Devotional Commentary</u>. Grand Rapids, MI: Eerdmans Publishing Co., 1970.

37. Thomas, W.H. Griffith. <u>Outline Studies in the Acts of the Apostles</u>. Grand Rapids, MI: Eerdmans Publishing Co., 1956.

38. Thomas, W.H. Griffith. <u>St. Paul's Epistle to the Romans</u>. Grand Rapids, MI: Eerdmans Publishing Co., 1946.

39. Thomas, W.H. Griffith. <u>Studies in Colossians & Philemon</u>. Grand Rapids, MI: Baker Book House, 1973.

40. <u>Tyndale New Testament Commentaries</u>. Grand Rapids, MI: Eerdmans Publishing Co., Began in 1958.

41. Walker, Thomas. <u>Acts of the Apostles</u>. Chicago, IL: Moody Press, 1965.

42. Walvoord, John. <u>The Thessalonian Epistles</u>. Grand Rapids, MI: Zondervan Publishing House, 1973.

The
Preacher's
Outline
&
Sermon
Bible®

"
Woe to me if I do not preach the gospel!

" (1 Cor. 9:16 NIV)

MATTHEW 6:5-6

L. The Right Motive for Prayer[DS1,2,3] (Part I), 6:5-6

1 **The wrong motive: Praying to be seen by men**
   a. Place: Loving to pray
      1) Only in the synagogue
      2) Only in the streets
   b. Reason: For recognition
   c. Reward: Man's esteem

2 **The right motive: Praying to be heard by God**
   a. Place: In one's private place
   b. Reason: God is in one's secret or private place[DS4]
   c. Reward: Will receive open blessings

5 "And when you pray, do not be like the hypocrites, for they love to pray standing in the synagogues and on the street corners to be seen by men. I tell you the truth, they have received their reward in full.

6 But when you pray, go into your room, close the door and pray to your Father, who is unseen. Then your Father, who sees what is done in secret, will reward you.

DIVISION IV

THE TEACHINGS OF THE MESSIAH TO
HIS DISCIPLES:
THE GREAT SERMON ON THE MOUNT,
5:1-7:29

L. THE RIGHT MOTIVE FOR PRAYER (PART I), 6:5-6

(6:5-6) *Introduction—Prayer—Motive:* this passage is speaking to *those who pray*—people who take prayer seriously. Prayer is one of the greatest acts of the Christian believer. Talking to God, whether by thought or tongue, is the way a believer fellowships with God; and the one thing God desires is fellowship with man (Is. 43:10). Thus, it is essential that we pray and pray often, sharing all day long.

However, that we *do* pray is not the concern of Christ in this point. His concern is *how* we pray. It is possible to pray amiss, with the wrong motive and in the wrong way. It is possible to pray and never be heard by God. It is possible to pray and to be speaking only to ourselves, to have our prayer go no higher than our own ears. Therefore, Christ sets out to teach us the right and wrong motives for praying.

1. The wrong motive: praying to be seen by men (v. 5).
2. The right motive: praying to be heard by God (v. 6).

DEEPER STUDY #1

(6:5-6) **Prayer:** there are dangers surrounding prayer, some negative factors that must be guarded against.

1. Prayer can become hypocritical (v. 5). A person can pray for the wrong reasons, with the wrong motives.
2. Prayer can become habit-forming (v. 5). Prayer is a wonderful experience, very rewarding emotionally and mentally and in having our needs met as God answers our prayer. We can begin to *love praying* and still be praying amiss.
3. Prayer can become connected with certain places (v. 5). A believer has places that mean much to him in his prayer life, but he must guard against limiting God's presence only to those places, even if it is the church.
4. Prayer can become empty repetition (v. 7). A person can take any phrase or form of prayer and make it a meaningful experience, or make it a formal and meaningless occasion. (Note how often the Lord's Prayer is repeated by rote memory with the mind focused elsewhere.)
5. Prayer can become too long (v. 7). A believer can begin to feel he is heard because of "many words" (cp. Eccl. 5:1-2).
6. Prayer can become self-glorifying (v. 8). A person can begin to feel he must inform and convince God of his *great* need. When the answer comes (out of the mercy of God, despite praying amiss), the believer begins to *glory in his spirituality*—that he has what it takes to get things from God.
7. Prayer can become self-deceptive (v. 7-8). A person can begin to think he is heard (1) because of "much speaking" and (2) because he convinces God of his need.

DEEPER STUDY #2

(6:5-6) *Prayer:* note several things.

1. Christ says "When you pray." He is referring to personal prayer (cp. v. 6).
2. Christ assumes that the believer does pray, and the idea conveyed is that the believer prays often.
3. Christ says there is a right way and a wrong way to pray. "When you pray, do not...." vs. "But when you pray...."
4. Christ says that some "love to pray," and they are the very ones who commit this fault. They pray amiss, with the wrong motive.
5. Christ pictures two men praying. One man prays to men (v. 5); the other man prays to the Father (v. 6). The first man is a hypocrite; the second man is a true son of the Father.

DEEPER STUDY #3

(6:5-6) *Prayer:* believers are expected to pray. Prayer is God's appointed medium through which He acts for man. *Sharing and talking* together are the way all persons communicate, fellowship, and commune together. This is true both with men and God. Prayer requires our presence, sharing, and talking; and God wants to fellowship and commune with us. Few persons heed this fact; few persons take prayer' seriously. Therefore, if we want the blessings of God upon our lives and ministries—if we want the work of God going forth in power and bearing fruit— we must pray and we must intercede in prayer.

But when you pray, go into your room close the door and pray to your Father, who is unseen. Then your Father, who sees what is done in secret, will reward you. (Mt. 6:6; cp. Mt. 6:7)

"This, then, is how you should pray: 'Our Father in heaven, hallowed be your name, (Mt. 6:9)

"Watch and pray so that you will not fall into temptation. The spirit is willing, but the body is weak." (Mt. 26:41; cp. Mk. 13:33; 14:38; Lk. 21:36; 22:40, 46)

Then Jesus told his disciples a parable to show them that they should always pray and not give up. (Lk. 18:1)

And pray in the Spirit on all occasions with all kinds of prayers and requests. With this in mind, be alert and always keep on praying for all the saints. (Eph. 6:18)

Pray continually; (1 Th. 5:17)

I want men everywhere to lift up holy hands in prayer, without anger or disputing. (1 Tim. 2:8)

1 (6:5) ***Prayer—Motive:*** the wrong motive for prayer is praying to be seen by men. Two preliminary things need to be looked at before discussing this point.

1. Praying—even loving to pray—is not a sign that a person really knows God.
2. The fact that a person really knows God means that he does pray. No matter what a man may think in his mind, if he really knows God and really believes in God, he talks to God. There is nothing that could keep him from praying. He knows God personally—knows Him as his Father who loves and cares for him ever so deeply. Therefore, just as any child who truly loves his father, the believer talks, converses, and shares with his Father. This says something to the person who prays primarily in public and prays little, if any, in private. He must search the genuineness of his heart and profession.

Christ says that a man who prays to be seen by men *loves to pray, but he is a hypocrite.*

1. The places where he *loves* to pray are *out in public,* in the synagogue (church), and in the streets (restaurants, and other public places.)

Thought 1. Note five lessons.
1) Some love to pray publicly. They love representing the group and vocalizing their praise and needs to God. Some have become very charismatic and fluent at public prayer, yet they lack that essential love for private praying. Christ says, "hypocrite" (v. 5).

2) Some pray only in public. They pray before their family (at meals and family prayers, usually with children); in church (when called upon); and in public (when eating in restaurants). They seldom, if ever, pray in private. How destitute is the prayer life of so many!

3) Prayer is to be offered to God both in church and in public. But public prayer is to be public, not private. Too often a person has his *personal devotions* when called upon to pray publicly. He has neglected his *private prayers* and his inner need has not been met. Thus when he begins to pray publicly, he slips into praying his own *private prayer* instead of representing the group.

4) Some hypocrites pray, and they pray much. There are some *religious people* who pray little, if any. These can learn from the hypocrites.

5) Note the posture of this hypocrite. He stood praying. This is an acceptable posture for prayer (Mk. 11:25); but the picture is that of pride, arrogance, and self-confidence. Kneeling is a picture of humility, reverence, and dependence upon God (Lk. 22:41; Eph. 3:14).

Living in harmony with one another. Do not be proud, but be willing to associate with people of low position. Do not be conceited. (Rom. 12:16)

If anyone thinks he is something when he is nothing, he deceives himself. (Gal. 6:3)

> For everything in the world—the cravings of sinful man, the lust of his eyes and the boasting of what he has and does—comes not from the Father but from the world. (1 John 2:16)
>
> "See, he is puffed up; his desires are not upright—but the righteous will live by his faith —(Hab. 2:4)

2. The man who prays only in public prays for only one reason: not because he loves to pray but because he loves recognition.

Thought 1. Note two lessons.

1. The sin is not failing to pray. The sin is praying *only* in church and in public. A person who prays publicly but seldom prays privately fools himself. Christ says real prayer (prayer to the Father) matters nothing to that person. He prays only for recognition—to be heard by men.

2. Praying publicly should be done. There is a great danger, however, in public prayer: having one's pride stroked. It is so easy to be praying publicly and have self-centered thoughts run across one's mind.

   ⇨ That one is really praying a good prayer. Such prayer is nothing but waxing eloquent with words.

   ⇨ That one's prayer will surely be admired.

   ⇨ That one's prayer is really demonstrating a close walk with God (a deep spirituality).

> *You hypocrites! Isaiah was right when he prophesied about you: "These people honor me with their lips, but their hearts are far from me. (Mt. 15:7-8)*
>
> *The man who thinks he knows something does not yet know as he ought to know. (1 Cor. 8:2)*
>
> *When pride comes, then comes disgrace, but with humility comes wisdom. (Prov. 11:2)*
>
> *Pride goes before destruction, a haughty spirit before a fall. (Prov. 16:18)*
>
> *Woe to those who are wise in their own eyes and clever in their own sight. (Isa. 5:21)*

3. The man who prays only in public receives his reward: public recognition. Three things need to be clearly seen about this man.

   a. He will experience good feelings and satisfying thoughts about his spiritual state and religious piety. He will possess a good self-image and some confidence in his standing with God. The esteem and praise of men and feeling good about what he has done gives him a good self-image. *But* in this case it is a false self-image.

   b. He has cheated himself, really missed out on the most intimate presence and greatest future in the universe. He has lost his soul. He shall never hear, "Well done thou good and faithful servant" (Mt. 25:21).

   c. He gets just what he deserves: public recognition. If he places so little value upon sharing with God Himself, he deserves no more than what man can give him—human recognition.

Thought 1. Man's esteem fails at several points.

1) Man's esteem is temporary. Everything passes–ever so quickly. Man soon forgets and moves on to other things.

2) Man's esteem becomes commonplace. Even the greatest skills that elicit praise become routine and commonplace to man when performed day by day. Soon man no longer acknowledges his uniqueness. Such abilities are merely expected and accepted; he no longer elicits praise and recognition.

3) Man's esteem is powerless. It cannot answer prayer; it can only recognize man's ability to put words together and to see man's expression, fervency, and emotion. Its power is limited to the things of this world, and that power is even limited and short lived. Man's esteem can do absolutely nothing about the spiritual needs of his heart.

4) Man's esteem is not to be the judge of his life—God is. No man is any greater than any other man; men are mere men. All men have the same need: to turn to God in prayer, praying for His acceptance and recognition. Therefore, the esteem of man *by men* is meaningless in light of judgment and eternity.

> *For, "All men are like grass, and all their glory is like the flowers of the field; the grass withers and the flowers fall, (1 Pet. 1:24)*

> *But man, despite his riches, does not endure; he is like the beasts that perish. (Psa. 49:12)*
>
> *For he will take nothing with him when he dies, his splendor will not descend with him. (Psa. 49:17)*
>
> *The more the priests increased, the more they sinned against me; they exchanged their Glory for something disgraceful. (Hosea 4:7)*

2 (5:6) **Prayer—Motive:** the right motive for prayer is praying to be heard by God. Three preliminary things need to be looked at in this point.

1. The willingness to take time to pray· "When you pray." There has to be the will to pray. The believer must take time to get alone to pray. Too few ever take time to pray, and even fewer spend more than a few minutes in prayer. Too many stay all wrapped up in the world and its day-to-day affairs, some of which are necessary, but how much more necessary is prayer!
2. A closet is a necessity. The believer must have a private place deliberately chosen for prayer.
3. A personal relationship with God: a *Father-son* relationship is absolutely essential. God is our *Father;* He is available as fathers are available to their children. We are to go to Him, pray, share, commune and let Him shower us with His care and protection and meet our every need (Ps. 91:1).

Note: Christ says that a man who is genuine prays to be heard by God and not by men.

1. The place he chooses for prayer is in his private closet. Christ says: "Get alone"; "Go into your room... close the door." Be unobserved, undisturbed, and unheard. (Cp. 2 Ki. 4:33; Is. 26:20.)

   a. *Get alone:* unobserved—out of everyone's sight.

   b. *Get alone:* undisturbed—avoid interruptions and disturbances.

   c. *Get alone:* unheard—concentrate and meditate to allow God the freedom to work in your heart as He wishes.

   > *About noon the following day as they were on their journey and approaching the city, Peter went up on the roof to pray. (Acts 10:9)*
   >
   > *Cornelius answered: "Four days ago I was in my house praying at this hour, at three in the afternoon. Suddenly a man in shining clothes stood before me (Acts 10:30)*
   >
   > *But when you pray, go into your room, close the door and pray to your Father, who is unseen. Then your Father, who sees what is done in secret, will reward you. (Mt. 6:6)*
   >
   > *Very early in the morning, while it was still dark, Jesus got up, left the house and went off to a solitary place, where he prayed. (Mark 1:35)*
   >
   > *After leaving them, he went up on a mountainside to pray. When evening came, the boat was in the middle of the lake, and he was alone on land. (Mark 6:46-47)*

> *One of those days Jesus went out to a mountainside to pray, and spent the night praying to God. (Luke 6:12)*
>
> *He withdrew about a stone's throw beyond them, knelt down and prayed, "Father, if you are willing, take this cup from me; yet not my will, but yours be done." (Luke 22:41-42)*

2. The reason the believer prays in his private closet is because God is in secret or unseen (see note–Mt. 6:4). Note two significant facts.

   a. God "is unseen"; therefore, a person can meet God only in *secret*. Even in the midst of a worshiping crowd, a person must concentrate and focus his attention upon God who is unseen. There must be a secret heart-to-heart meeting and communion if a person wishes to pray and truly share with God.

   b. God "is unseen"; therefore, He is not interested in, show, but in substance. Show is before men. Substance is found in the secret, quiet, meditative place. Remember: everything that exists began with an idea, and the development of the idea came from *private and quiet thought and meditation,* not out in the public before people—at least not often. The same is true of spiritual matters. Spiritual show takes place before people, but spiritual substances or qualities that really matter take place in secret. When the believer pours out his heart, he receives his greatest encouragement and strength in the secret place of the Most High, not in the public places of mere man.

Thought 1. Many pray on the run; few pray in secret. Why do so few have a quiet time, a daily worship and devotional time? Why do so few keep their daily appointment with God? This is one of the most difficult things in the world to understand in light of who God is and in light of man's desperate plight and need. No man would ever fail to keep his appointment with the state leader of his nation.

1) Many say they do not have the time, so they do not take the time. But in all honesty, it takes only a little effort to get up a while earlier in the morning—if they are really all that pressed for time. All they need to do is to rearrange their schedule to allow for a quiet time just as they arrange for any other important meeting. However, few do this; therefore, they are without excuse. Many believers are faithful in meeting God daily. It is just a matter of discipline and priority.

2) Most have the time; they just do not take the time. They neglect getting alone with God consistently.

3) Many have not been taught the importance and benefit of a quiet time with God every day. This is a justified accusation against Christian parents, preachers, and teachers. So few have practiced and stressed what they have always heard about the importance of prayer. The silence of believers and their failure to reach the world in sound doctrine is unbelievable, especially after two thousand years.

4) Some have not yet learned to discipline themselves and to be consistent in their spiritual lives. There is no better area to learn discipline and consistency than in a daily quiet time. A person should just begin and do it. When a day is missed, a person should flee discouragement, "forgetting what is behind," and reach forth to a new day and begin again. Eventually, consistency and discipline will be learned, and the person's soul will be fed with the "unsearchable riches of Christ" (Eph.3:8, 20; cp. Ph.3:13).

3. The reward of the genuine prayer warrior is open blessings. The praying believer will be rewarded in two very special ways.

a. The strength and presence of God will be upon his life (Ezra 8:22; 1 Pet. 5:6). God's presence is unmistakable. There is a difference between a person who walks in God's presence and a life that walks only in this world (Mt. 6:25-34, esp. 33). God rewards the praying believer with His presence and blessings. The believer's needs, material and spiritual, are met day by day.

b. The believer's prayers will also be answered (Mt. 21:22; Jn. 16:24; 1 Jn. 5:14-15). The answers to prayer are clearly seen by a thinking and honest observer. God has promised to answer the true prayer of a genuine believer. God takes care of the genuine believer with a very special care. Sometimes the answer is seen in a renewed strength.

Now to him who is able to do immeasurably more than all we ask or imagine, according to his power that is at work within us,
(Eph. 3:20)

- in a provision of some necessity.

But seek first his kingdom and his righteousness, and all these things will be given to you as well. (Mt. 6:33)

- in a conquest of some great temptation or trial.

No temptation has seized you except what is common to man. And God is faithful; he will not let you be tempted beyond what you can bear. But when you are tempted, he will also provide a way out so that you can stand up under it. (1 Cor. 10:13)

- in a peace that passes and transcends all human understanding.

Do not be anxious about anything, but in everything, by prayer and petition, with thanksgiving, present your requests to God. And the peace of God, which transcends all understanding, will guard your hearts and your minds in Christ Jesus. (Phil. 4:6-7)

- in self-discipline that is incomprehensible.

For God did not give us a spirit of timidity, but a spirit of power, of love and of self-discipline. (2 Tim. 1:7)

Thought 1. The praying believer, the believer who becomes a true intercessor, will be rewarded openly on that special day of redemption.

1) God "was appalled that there was no one to intervene [no intercessor]" (Isa. 59:16).
2) Christ, the Great Intercessor, "always lives to intercede for them" (Heb. 7:25).
3) The interceding believer shall stand openly in a very special relationship with Jesus, the Great Intercessor Himself, before God the Father.

If you believe, you will receive whatever you ask for in prayer. (Mt. 21:22)

"So I say to you: Ask and it will be given to you; seek and you will find; knock and the door will be opened to you." (Lk. 11:9)

And I will do whatever you ask in my name, so that the Son may bring glory to the Father. You may ask me for anything in my name, and I will do it. (Jn. 14:13-14)

If you remain in me and my words remain in you, ask whatever you wish, and it will be given you. (Jn. 15:7)

Until now you have not asked for anything in my name. Ask and you will receive, and your joy will be complete. (Jn. 16:24)

And receive from him anything we ask, because we obey his commands and do what pleases him. (1 Jn. 3:22)

This is the confidence we have in approaching God: that if we ask anything according to his will, he hears us. And if we know that he hears us—whatever we ask—we know that we have what we asked of him. (1 Jn. 5:14-15)

DEEPER STUDY #4

(6:6) **Prayer:** prayer is to be done secretly. The believer is to get by himself and pray to God secretly. This means three things:

1. Concentration is needed: meditation, contemplation, thinking deeply upon God and sharing accordingly.
2. A person must get alone, apart from all else: secluded, private, out of view from all.
3. God is unseen: invisible, yet there. A person must believe and have faith that God is there. God is Spirit, but He still hears and responds. Every believer should have a secret, quiet place that is dear to his heart, dear because it is the place where he draws near to God and God draws near to him. (See Deeper Study #3 – Jn. 1:48.)

MATTHEW 6:7-8

	M. The Three Great Rules for Prayer, (Part II) 6:7-8
1 Rule 1: Do not use meaningless repetition[DS1] **2 Rule 2: Do not speak much**	7 And when you pray, do not keep on babbling like pagans, for they think they will be heard because of their many words.
3 Rule 3: Trust God a. He knows your needs b. He desires to hear your prayer	8 Do not be like them, for your Father knows what you need before you ask him.

The Teachings of the Messiah to
His Disciples:
The Great Sermon on the Mount,
5:1-7:29

M. The Three Great Rules for Prayer (Part II), 6:7-8

(6:7-8) **Introduction:** among the religious there is often a tendency toward long prayers, particularly in public. Too often people measure prayer by its fluency and length, thinking that length means devotion. "Be not rash with thy mouth, and let not thine heart be hasty to utter anything before God; for God is in heaven, and thou upon earth; therefore let thy words be few" (Eccl. 5:2). Christ puts the matter very simply, yet strongly: "When you pray," follow three great rules.

1. Rule 1: do not use empty repetition (v.7).
2. Rule 2: do not speak much (v.7).
3. Rule 3: trust God (v.8).

1 (6:7) **Prayer—Repetition:** the first great rule of prayer is striking—do not use empty repetition (see DEEPER STUDY #1 – Mt. 6:7). There are several things that lend themselves to empty repetition.

1. Memorized prayer: just saying the words of a form prayer, for example, the Lord's prayer. There is nothing wrong with praying a memorized prayer, but it should be prayed through and not just repeated with no thought behind the words.

2. Written, well-worded prayers: thinking that what we say is so expressive and so well worded that it is bound to carry weight with God. The words may be descriptive and beautifully arranged, but the heart must be offering the prayer, not the mind and ego. Such prayer is empty repetition.

3. Ritual prayer: saying the same prayer at the same time on the same occasion—over and over again. This can soon become empty repetition.

4. Formal worship: praying in the same way on a rigid schedule can lead to praying by habit (repeated practice) with little or no meaning to it.

5. Thoughtless prayer: speaking words while our minds are wandering. Being tired is no excuse. It is better not to pray than to pray insincerely.

6. Religious words and phrases: using certain words or phrases over and over in prayer (just because they are religious sounding). (Compare using such words over and over as *mercy, grace, I thank thee O God, in Jesus' name.*)

7. Habitual references to God: using such empty repetition as "Lord this," and "Lord that," and "Lord here," and "Lord there," and "Lord…," "Lord…," "Lord…" How little thought is really given to approaching Him whose name is "Wonderful, Counselor, The Mighty God, The Everlasting Father, The Prince of Peace" (Isa. 9:6).

There are several things that will keep us from

using empty repetition in prayer.

1.   A genuine heart: really knowing God personally and having a moment-by-moment fellowship with Him all day long.
2.   Thought and concentration: really focusing upon what we are saying.
3.   Desire for fellowship with God: praying sincerely, really meaning it.
4.   Preparation: preparing ourselves for prayer by first meditating in God's Word.

Note something of extreme importance in discussing "babbling" repetition. Christ does not say repetition in prayer is wrong. It is not wrong. What is wrong is vain, empty, meaningless, foolish repetition. Christ Himself used repetition in prayer (Mt. 26:44), so did Daniel (Dan. 9:18-19), and so did the Psalmist (Ps. 136: 1f).

Thought 1. Note six lessons.

1)   There is one major problem with the praying of believers: they do not pray enough. They do not take enough time to pray and to pray in earnest. There is one major problem *when believers do pray:* prayer is often vain, empty, thoughtless, meaningless, and repetitive. Too often a believer prays and does not concentrate. His mind wanders off somewhere else; he only mouths the words. Such thoughtless and meaningless prayer is clearly seen in public prayer and in the powerlessness of believers today.

2)   There is one sure way to prepare our hearts for prayer: meditating in God's Word.

All Scripture is God-breathed and is useful for teaching, rebuking, correcting and training in righteousness. (2 Tim. 3:16)

It is in the Scripture that the believer learns about God, himself, and the world—the nature and truth of all things. It is the Spirit of God who takes the Word of God and moves upon the believer's heart revealing that for which the believer should pray. Therefore, the believer is stirred to pray for whatever the Word of God and the Spirit of God has shown him (Rom. 8:26; cp. Jn. 14:26; 16:13; 1 Cor. 2:12-13).

3) Meaningless repetition in prayer, whether formal or thoughtless, is *desensitizing.*
   ⇨ It discourages the sincere and the newly converted.
   ⇨ It cools the willing and the gifted.
   ⇨ It stifles the committed and the mature.
   ⇨ It turns away the seeking and the lost.

4) Repetition in prayer *is* dull. Empty repetition affects worship, interest, and attendance at services.

5) Meaningless repetition is tragic. Prayer should be one of the most meaningful experiences in life. God is certainly willing to meet the believer in a very special way—anytime, any place. So many hearts are just...
   • barren   • lethargic
   • dull   • desert-like
   • complacent   • rusted
   • dry   • still
   • hard

So much praying is merely going over and over the same things ranging from "bless Mom and Dad" to "give us a good day tomorrow."

6) Empty repetition turns God away and cuts the heart of the committed.

"Having a form of godliness but denying its power. Have nothing to do with them." (2 Tim. 3:5)

"You hypocrites! Isaiah was right when he prophesied about you: These people honor me with their lips, but their hearts are far from me." (Mt. 15:7-8)

DEEPER STUDY #1

(6:7) *Prayer—Repetition, Meaningless* (battologesete): to babble much; to use many phrases; to say idle things; to say meaningless things. Meaningless repetition means at least two things.

1. It means saying the same words over and over again without putting one's heart and thought into what is being said.
2. It means using certain religious words or phrases (sometimes over and over again) and thinking God hears because one is using such religious talk.

2 (6:7) *Prayer, Long:* the second great rule of prayer is an eye-opener—do not speak much. Too many think that length equals devotion; that is, the longer they pray the more God will listen to them (they are showing God their sincerity), and the more spiritual they will become.

God does not hear a person's prayer because it is long, but because his heart is genuinely poured out to God. Length has nothing to do with devotion, but a sincere heart does.

Long prayers are not forbidden. What is forbidden is the idea that long prayers are automatically heard by God. Christ prayed all night (Lk. 6:12). The early disciples prayed and fasted, and sought God for ten days and nights waiting for the coming of the Holy Spirit (Acts 2: 1f), A believer should sense the needs of the world so much that he is driven to seek God and His intervention for long periods of time, and the seeking should be often (Eph. 6:18).

Why do some pray long prayers?

1. Some feel long prayers convince God. They feel God has to be moved, nudged, and stirred to hear and answer.
2. Some feel they need long prayers to explain the situation. They feel God needs to be informed and made to understand a particular situation and how it has affected them.
3. Some feel long prayers make them more spiritual, more mature, and more devoted.
4. Some feel long prayers are just demanded of believers. It is expected; it is the religious and godly thing to do.
5. Some feel long prayers show God their sincerity. They secure God's approval by long prayers.
6. Some feel long prayers impress people. They show people just how deeply spiritual they really are.

What are ways to prevent the sins that arise from long prayers?

Do not be quick with your mouth, do not be hasty in your heart to utter anything before God. God is in heaven and you are on earth, so let your words be few. (Eccl 5:2)

1. "Do not be quick with your mouth." Control your mouth. Do not let your mouth rattle on and on without thought. It will often rush and hurry with every thought that crosses your mind.
2. Do not be "hasty in your heart to utter anything before God": sit still, be quiet, without saying a word for awhile. Do not rush forward to speak.
3. Think about who God is. Picture a man: his mouth is quiet; he has been still for some time. He has been preparing, gaining control of his mind and thoughts so he can appear before the Sovereign Majesty of the universe. He focuses his thoughts upon God, the One who is in heaven far above the earth. He meditates upon God's sovereignty and majesty. God is the center of his thoughts (Ps. 46: 10).
4. "Let your words be few." Speak—but make your words deliberate—just as deliberate as the words of any interviewer before a sovereign ruler. Request—just as any obedient son would request of a revered father. The person who approaches God like this speaks with respect and thought, with care and love.

He speaks few words and straight to the point—all from a prepared heart and mind.

When should the believer spend a long time in prayer? There *are* special times when an extended prayer time is necessary. Some of the times are clearly seen in Scripture.

1. Sometimes a special pull to praise and adore God is felt within. When the believer feels this pull, he should get alone, spending a long time praising and worshiping God (cp. Acts 16:25).
2. Sometimes a special need arises. This may be the believer's own need or a friend's need. He should intercede until God gives the assurance that the need will be met (Eph. 6:18; cp. Acts 12:1-5, esp. v. 5).
3. Sometimes an unusual experience or event has taken place or is about to take place in the believer's life or ministry. He should get alone and share the event with God. And he should stay before God until the experience has taken place (courage, confidence, power, faith, love). (See Introduction – Mt. 4:1-11.)
4. Sometimes a great trial or temptation is faced. A long session of prayer may be needed to gain strength and to keep the believer away from the trial or temptation. (See DEEPER STUDY #1 – Mt.4:1-11.)
5. Sometimes a matter needs to be worked through or a major decision needs to be made. Help and direction should be sought from God. God should be acknowledged in all of the

believer's ways. He should remain before God until the answer is given. (Cp. Acts 13:1-3, esp. 2.)

Thought 1. Prayer is a matter of the heart, not a matter of words and length. Praying is sharing; it is sharing with God just like a person shares with any other person. Just as he shares thoughts, feelings, praise, and requests with others, so he shares with God.

Thought 2. Prayer is a personal relationship. Prayer is not speaking into thin air. God may be "unseen" (v. 6); He may be invisible, but He is there. He is there more than any other person who may be in our presence. He is the One whom all men are to know and to whom all men are to be vitally related. Too often, the awareness and consciousness of His presence are allowed to fade, and we just go through our long prayer with a wandering mind leaping from thought to thought. Long prayers lend themselves to this danger. How insincere! How irreverent! How often the heart of God must be cut and hurt!

Thought 3. There are prayers of believers and prayers of the heathen. A distinction is made by Christ Himself. He says that both pray.
1) The heathen pray using meaningless repetition and speaking empty words.
2) The believer is vitally related to God; therefore, he prays to God who is his Father. He prays to God just as a son shares with his revered father.

And when you pray, do not keep on babbling like pagans, for they think they will be heard because of their many words. (Mt. 6:7)

All man's efforts are for his mouth, yet his appetite is never satisfied. (Eccl. 6:7)

3 (6:8) **Prayer:** the third great rule of prayer is forceful—trust God.

1. God knows the believer's need even before the believer asks. Why then should the believer pray?

Prayer demonstrates our need for God and our dependence upon God. Prayer gives time for concentrated sharing and communion between the believer and God. It is not enough for man to carry a knowledge of God in his mind as he walks through life. Man needs to have times when he is in the presence of God and can concentrate his thoughts and fellowship upon God. He needs such time with God just as he needs such time with his family and friends. Man is not meant to live in isolation from people nor from God. He must have times when he is in the presence of both man and God and can concentrate his thoughts and attention upon both.

The believer, therefore, does not pray only to have his needs met but to share and fellowship and to enrich his life with God.

Thought 1. God knows the believer's needs. The believer does not have to worry about God's knowing or meeting his needs. The believer's concern should be living in the presence of God, taking enough time to share and to fellowship with God. The more he shares and fellowships with God, the more he will know God and learn to trust and to depend upon God's care and promises.

Thought 2. God is the believer's Father. The believer is God's son. The believer can, therefore, *rest* in God and His promises. He does not have to strain and pray long in order for his Father to hear him. His Father already knows and cares. He is to get with His Father for long periods of time sharing and fellowshipping, learning and getting to know his Father intimately.

2. God desires to hear. God knows the believer's need even before the believer asks (cp. 2 Chron. 16:9; Isa. 65:24). God desires to hear and answer the believer's prayer, to meet the believer's needs. God desires to work for the believer's deliverance and salvation (see outline and notes Rom. 8:23-27; 8:28-39. This is one of the great passages on assurance and confidence.)

3. God has ordained prayer as the medium through which He blesses and moves among men. (See DEEPER STUDY #3, <u>Prayer</u> – Mt. 6:5-6; pt. 2– 1 Th. 5:15-22).

How great is your goodness, which you have stored up for those who fear you, which you bestow in the sight of men on those who take refuge in you. (Psa. 31:19)

Many are the woes of the wicked, but the Lord's unfailing love surrounds the man who trusts in him. (Psa. 32:10)

The LORD redeems his servants; no one will be condemned who takes refuge in him. (Psa. 34:22)

A song of ascents. Those who trust in the LORD are like Mount Zion, which cannot be shaken but endures forever. (Psa. 125:1)

Trust in the LORD with all your heart and lean not on your own understanding; in all your ways acknowledge him, and he will make your paths straight. (Prov. 3:5-6)

Fear of man will prove to be a snare, but whoever trusts in the LORD is kept safe. (Prov. 29:25)

You will keep in perfect peace him whose mind is steadfast, because he trusts in you. Trust in the Lord forever, for the Lord, the Lord, is the Rock eternal. (Isa. 26:3-4)

"But blessed is the man who trusts in the LORD, whose confidence is in him. He will be like a tree planted by the water that sends out its roots by the stream. It does not fear when heat comes; its leaves are always green. It has no worries in a year of drought and never fails to bear fruit." (Jer. 17:7-8)

MATTHEW 6:9-13

N. The Model Prayer[DS1]
(Part III), 6:9-13
(Lk. 11:2-4)

1 There is surrender
  a. To our Father[DS2] in heaven[DS3]
  b. To God's holy name[DS4]

2 There is a request & plea
  a. For God's kingdom[DS5]
  b. For God's will[DS6]
  c. For daily bread[DS7]
  d. For forgiveness[DS8]
  e. For deliverance[DS9]

3 There is praise & commitment[DS10]

9 "This, then, is how you should pray: 'Our Father in heaven, hallowed be your name,
10 Your kingdom come, your will be done on earth as it is in heaven.
11 Give us today our daily bread.
12 Forgive us our debts, as we also have forgiven our debtors.
13 And lead us not into temptation, but deliver us from the evil one.'

N. THE MODEL PRAYER (PART III), 6:9-13

(6:9-13) *Introduction—Prayer—Lord's Prayer:* What is the Lord's prayer? Is it a prayer to be recited as it so often is—just by memory, or just as a form prayer?

Note the words "This, then, is how you should pray." Note also Luke's account where the disciples asked Jesus to teach them to pray (Lk. 11: 1-2). The prayer was given to show the disciples *how to* pray—how they should go about praying, not the *words* they should pray. The very context of what Christ had just taught shows this clearly (cp. Mt. 6:5-8).

The Lord's prayer is a model prayer that is to be *prayed through.* It is "how you should pray," *in this way, like this,* that a person is to pray. Christ was teaching the disciples how to pray. He was giving words, phrases, thoughts that are to be the points of the believer's prayer. The believer is to develop the points as he prays. An example would be something like this:

⇨ "Our Father...": "Thank you, Father, that you are our Father—that you have adopted us as children of God, sons and daughters of yours. Thank you for the believers of the world who make up the family of God. Thank you for the church, the body of Christ that gives us the family of God. Thank you for loving us that much." And on and on the believer is to pray.

⇨ "...in heaven": "Thank you for heaven—that you are in heaven—that you have chosen us to be with you in heaven, Thank you, Father, for the hope and anticipation of heaven." And on and on the believer prays.

Christ taught His disciples to pray "like this." When the believer prays through the Lord's prayer, he finds he has covered the scope of what God wants him to pray. How much pain the Lord's heart must bear because of the way man has abused and misused His prayer! How desperately believers need to pray through the Lord's prayer! How desperately the *prophets and teachers* of the world need to pray as Christ taught! How much you and all of us as ministers of God need to preach and teach that the Lord's prayer is to be *prayed through* and not just recited.

1. There is surrender and acknowledgment (v. 9).
2. There is request and plea (v. 10- 13).
3. There is praise and commitment (v. 13).

DEEPER STUDY #1

(6:9-13) *Prayer:* What is prayer?

1. Prayer is sharing and fellowshipping with God (Mt. 6:9). It is enough for a person to have a knowledge of God as he walks through life. He needs to have times when he can get alone with God to concentrate his thoughts and attention upon God. He needs such times with God just as he needs such times with his family and friends. Man was not made to live in isolation from people nor from God. He must have times when he is in the presence of both man and God and can concentrate his thoughts and attention upon both (see note—Mt. 6:8).

2. Prayer is surrendering to God (Mt. 6:9). The believer surrenders himself and his time to God. There is no such thing as prayer without a person and time. A person must submit himself to God before he wills to pray, and even then he must take the time to pray. A person who has surrendered himself to God and is surrendering or taking his time to talk with God is praying (see note 1—Mt. 6:9).

3. Prayer is requesting and pleading with God (Mt. 6:10). It is demonstrating one's need and dependence upon God. It is pouring out one's heart in need and trusting God to meet one's need.

4. Prayer is acknowledging and praising God (Mt. 6:9-10, 13). It is acknowledging God as the Sovereign and Majestic Lord to whom belongs the kingdom, the power, and the glory, forever.

1 (6:9) *Prayer—Surrender:* the believer's prayer is to be a surrender.

1. There is the surrender of the believer to God and to God's family.
   a. When a person genuinely says "Father," he is surrendering to God. He is...
      - denying humanism, self-sufficiency, and all other gods.
      - surrendering himself to the Father of the Lord Jesus Christ.
      - acknowledging the Father of the Lord Jesus Christ to be his own Father.
   b. When a person prays "<u>our</u> Father," a person is surrendering his independency and accepting God's family. He is assuming his responsibility in the family of God.

2. There is the surrender of the believer to *heaven,* the spiritual world or dimension of being. The believer surrenders and sets his mind and heart upon the Kingdom of God and His righteousness. His whole being is surrendered and committed to seeking the things of the spiritual world. (See outline and notes—Eph. 1: 3.)

3. There is the surrender of the believer to the holy name of God. The believer just bows in total and abject poverty, in nothingness before the holy name of God. He is swallowed up in the knowledge of the "hallowedness," the sovereignty and majesty of God's being. God is all and man is nothing! He is totally dependent upon God.

Note: when a person reaches this point of surrender, then he is ready to present his needs to God. He is ever so conscious that only God can meet his needs.

DEEPER STUDY #2

(6:9) *God-Father:* God is addressed as "Our Father." Father denotes a family relationship and shows three things.

1. It shows that "God [who is] ... in heaven" is the believer's Father. Thus, a relationship with the unseen heavenly world and the seen earthly world is established. God represents the unseen world and the believer represents the seen world. In the believer a whole new being is created (a new creature) and a whole new world is recognized and established: a world of the spirit and the physical, of the unseen and the seen, of heaven and earth (2 Cor. 5:17; Eph. 4:23-24; Col. 4:10. Especially see notes—Eph. 2:11-18; pt. 4— 2:14-15; 4:17.)

2. The word "Father" establishes a relationship between a believer and all other believers. All believers belong to the same family; they all have common interests, cares, and responsibilities within the family.

3. The word "Father" pinpoints God as the believer's source. God, as Father, is the Person who loves and provides and cares for the believer's needs, even as an earthly father looks after his child (Mt. 6:25-34, esp. 33; Lk. 11:11–13; Psa. 103:13; Mal. 3:17; cp. Heb. 2:18; 4:15-16).

Thought 1. "Our Father" is the first point to pray.
The believer is to pray like this.

⇨ "Father, thank you <u>for yourself:</u> that you are <u>our</u>
<u>Father</u>...."

⇨ "Thank you for adopting us as children of God:
that you have chosen us ...."

⇨ "Thank you for 'the household of faith,' for the
'family of God' ...."

Thought 2. The phrase "Our Father" says three
things about prayer.

1) The believer is not to pray alone—not always.
The word "our" shows this. Christ has just taught
that a person should pray alone. He now says
there are times when a person should pray with
others. God is "our Father."

2) The believer is taught to whom to pray: to God
and to Him alone.

3) The believer is taught to address God as "Father."
He is taught what his relationship to God is to be,
that of a child to a Father.

   *If you, then, though you are evil, know how to
   give good gifts to your children, how much more
   will your Father in heaven give good gifts to those
   who ask him! (Mt. 7:11)*

   *Since you call on a Father who judges each man's
   work impartially, live your lives as strangers here
   in reverent fear. (1 Pet. 1:17)*

Thought 3. God is "<u>our</u> Father." God has no
favorites: "God does **not show** favoritism" (Acts
10:34).

1) God is "our Father" by creation; that is, He is the
Father of all men everywhere because He is the

Creator of all men (Gen. 1:1; Mal. 2:10; Isa. 64:8; Acts 27:28).

2) God is "our Father" by recreation (2 Cor. 5:17) and adoption (see DEEPER STUDY #2—Gal. 4:5-6; cp. Eph. 1:5). He is "our Father" to all who believe in the Lord Jesus Christ and the redemption that is in Him (Eph. 2:19).

For you did not receive a spirit that makes you a slave again to fear, but you received the Spirit of sonship. And by him we cry, "Abba, Father." (Rom. 8:15)

But when the time had fully come, God sent his Son, born of a woman, born under law, (Gal. 4:4)

To redeem those under law, that we might receive the full rights of sons. (Gal. 4:5)

Because you are sons, God sent the Spirit of his Son into our hearts, the Spirit who calls out, "Abba, Father." (Gal. 4:6)

Thought 4. There is one time In particular when the believer must approach God as Father: when returning to God and repenting of sin (cp. the prodigal son, Lk. 15:18).

Thought 5. "Our Father" settles all the relationships in the world.

1) It settles a person's relationship with himself. Every person fails and comes short, and sometimes he' gets down on himself. He feels like a failure— hopeless, helpless, worthless, useless. "Our Father" says that such a person matters; he always matters to God. He can come to the Father and share his concerns.

2) It settles a person's relationship with others (see Thought 3).

DEEPER STUDY #3

(6:9) *Heaven:* the word is plural in the Greek, heavens. The New Testament speaks of at least three heavens:

⇨ the atmosphere surrounding the earth (cp. Mt. 6:26, "the birds of the heaven").

⇨ the outer space of heavenly bodies (cp. Mt. 24:29; Rev. 6:13).

⇨ the place above and beyond the physical dimension of being where God's presence is fully manifested. In modern language "the above and beyond" is another dimension of being entirely; it is the *spiritual world, another dimension of being.* It is a spiritual world where God's presence is fully manifested, and where Christ and His followers live awaiting the glorious day of redemption. That glorious day of redemption is the day when God shall take the imperfect heavens and earth (the physical dimension) and transform them into the new heavens and earth (the spiritual and eternal dimension). (See note— 2 Pet. 3:8-10, esp. 3:11-14 for more discussion.)

Thought 1. "Our Father in Heaven" is the second point to be prayed. The believer is to pray like this:

⇨ "Father, thank you for heaven: the hope, the anticipation of heaven...."

⇨ "Thank you that you are in heaven...."

⇨ "Thank you for your promise that we shall be where you are..." (Jn. 17:24).

Thought 2. Note several lessons.

1) The believer must direct his prayers to heaven. God's throne is in heaven (Ps. 103:19), and it is before the throne of God that Christ is appearing as the Advocate or Mediator for the believer.

But Stephen, full of the Holy Spirit, looked up to heaven and saw the glory of God, and Jesus standing at the right hand of God. (Acts 7:55)

"Look," he said, "I see heaven open and the Son of Man standing at the right hand of God." (Acts 7:56)

For there is one God and one mediator between God and men, the man Christ Jesus, (1 Tim. 1:5)

The point of what we are saying is this: We do have such a high priest, who sat down at the right hand of the throne of the Majesty in heaven, (Heb. 8:1)

But the ministry Jesus has received is as superior to theirs as the covenant of which he is mediator is superior to the old one, and it is founded on better promises. (Heb 8:6)

For this reason Christ is the mediator of a new covenant, that those who are called may receive the promised eternal inheritance—now that he has died as a ransom to set them free from the sins committed under the first covenant. (Heb. 9:15)

2) How should we approach God? The words "Our Father in heaven" tell us.
   a. "Father" says that we can approach Him boldly to "find grace to help us in our time of need" (Heb. 4:16).
   b. "In heaven" says that we are to approach respectfully, in reverence and fear and awe (Ps. 111: 9; cp. Eccl. 5:2).

3) The heavens reveal the power and glory of God. Space shows His handiwork (Ps. 19:1; 150:1). When connected together, the words "Our Father" and the words "in heaven" put two great things together: the love of God and the power of God. God through love has become "our Father, " and "God in heaven" has shown His glorious power which is at the disposal of His child. The believer's Father has the power to do anything, even to hang the world in space (Eph. 3:20; Ps. 121:1-8)

4) The believer's true citizenship is in heaven (Ph. 3:20). God is there; the Lord Jesus is also there (Heb. 8:1; cp. Ps. 103:19). Therefore, the longing of the mature believer's heart is to be in heaven where His Father and His Lord are. He directs his attention, prayers, energy, and life toward heaven.

However, do not rejoice that the spirits submit to you, but rejoice that your names are written in heaven." (Luke 10:20)

In my Father's house are many rooms; if it were not so, I would have told you. I am going there to prepare a place for you. (John 14:2)

Now we know that if the earthly tent we live in is destroyed, we have a building from God, an eternal house in heaven, not built by human hands. (2 Cor. 5:1)

But our citizenship is in heaven. And we eagerly await a Savior from there, the Lord Jesus Christ, (Phil. 3:20)

The faith and love that spring from the hope that is stored up for you in heaven and that you have already heard about in the word of truth, the gospel (Col. 1:5)

For he was looking forward to the city with foundations, whose architect and builder is God. (Heb. 11:10)

5) God sees all from heaven (Ps. 33:13-19).
   ⇨ He sees all the sons of men.
   ⇨ He looks upon all the inhabitants of the earth.
   ⇨ He considers all their works.

However, there is one thing in particular that God sees: the person who fears Him and hopes in His mercy. He sees this person in order to deliver his soul from death (Ps. 33:18-19). This is one of the prime reasons the believer keeps his eyes upon heaven.

DEEPER STUDY #4

(6:9) *Hallowed* (hagiastheto): to be counted holy; to be treated holy; to be counted and treated as different. The prayer is for men to count and treat the name of God differently, to set His name apart from all other names (see note—1 Pet. 1:15-16).

Thought 1. "Hallowed be your name" is the third point to be prayed. The believer is to pray like this:
⇨ "Father, hallowed is your name. Your name is holy, set apart, different from all other names. There is none but you ... you and you alone. You are above, before, over all ...."

Thought 2. Note several lessons.
1) God's name is holy, righteous, pure. It is above, before, and over all names. Therefore, the believer's prayer is for God's name to be adored and honored by all men. (See outline and notes—Mt. 5:33-37 for a contrast in how some men treat the name of God.)

2) The first thing prayer should do is praise and glorify God. That is the point Christ is making in the words...
   • "Our Father...
   • in heaven...
   • hallowed be your name."

   God has done everything; He has made the world and given life to it. Man owes his very life to God. Therefore, the first thing man should do is praise God.

   Every good and perfect gift is from above, coming down from the Father of the heavenly lights, who does not change like shifting shadows. (James 1:17)

3) The first purpose of man is to glorify God by his life: "Be holy; because I am holy" (1 Pet. 1:15-16). Life includes speech; therefore, man should be praising God's holiness by word as well as by life. In fact, since the primary purpose of man is to be holy, then it follows that the first words spoken to God should be praising His holiness. All prayer should be centered around praising God for who He is—in all His holiness and fullness. His name is "hallowed," different, set apart from all other names. And thank God that His name is set apart, for imagine what life would be if His name should be no more than a man's name.

   If only for this life, we have hope in Christ, we are to be pitied more than all men. (1 Cor. 15:19)

4) God's glory is the very reason Christ came to earth (Jn.17:1-26, esp. vs.1, 4-6, 22-26). God says He shall be exalted in the earth even among the heathen (Ps. 46:10; cp. Ps. 2:1-5, esp. vs. 4-5), How much man needs to fix his mind upon the holiness and glory of God's name!

*For this is what the high and lofty One says—he who
lives forever, whose name is holy: "I live in a high
and holy place, but also with him who is contrite and
lowly in spirit, to revive the spirit of the lowly and to
revive the heart of the contrite. (Isa. 57:15)*

*And said: "Praise be to the name of God forever and
ever; wisdom and power are his. (Dan. 2:20)*

*"Be still, and know that I am God; I will be exalted
among the nations, I will be exalted in the earth."
(Ps. 46:10)*

5) Men praise and honor each other among themselves.
Men glorify men, even make idols of them (see note—
Mt. 6:2). Some are more loyal to the names of the
famous (athletes, stars, politicians) than they are to
the name of God. They are more disturbed when the
name of their idol is spoken of disrespectfully than
they are when the name of God is cursed. How
differently Scripture presents God's name: "Hallowed
be your name." God says that the man who curses
His name is to be judged severely (Ex. 20:7).

2 (6:10-13) **Prayer:** the believer is to request and
plea for several things (see DEEPER STUDIES
#5-9—Mt. 6:10, 6:11; 6:12; 6:13).

DEEPER STUDY #5

(6:10) *Kingdom of God:* see DEEPER STUDY
3—Mt. 19:23-24.

Thought 1. "Your kingdom come" is the first
request to be prayed. The believer is to pray like
this:

⇨ "Father, let your kingdom come right here on this earth. Let Christ rule and reign in the hearts and the lives of all. Send Him, His kingdom, His sovereignty right now. God, I pray, even so come Lord Jesus, come...."

Thought 2. The Kingdom of God is to be the focus of the believer's requests, the very first thing for which he asks. There are three reasons for this.

1) It is the very message that Jesus Christ and the early apostles, preached and taught and prayed (Mt. 3:2; 4:17; 5:3, 10, 19-20)

2) It is the very thing for which God longs. He longs for the day when He will rule and reign in the hearts of all men, perfectly—the day when all men will willingly submit and serve Him—the day when all thoughts, all words, all behavior will be exactly what they should be.

3) It is the very substance of the believer's life, or at least it should be. The believer should be living and loving and having his being for God and God alone. His whole focus and attention, energy and effort should be centered on the rule and reign of God on earth.

And saying, "Repent, for the kingdom of heaven is near." (Mt. 3:2)

From that time on Jesus began to preach, "Repent, for the kingdom of heaven is near." (Mt. 4:17)

"Blessed are the poor in spirit, for theirs is the kingdom of heaven. (Mt. 5:3)

Blessed are those who are persecuted because of righteousness, for theirs is the kingdom of heaven. (Mt. 5:10)

For the kingdom of God is not a matter of eating and drinking, but of righteousness, peace and joy in the Holy Spirit, (Rom. 14:17)

Thought 3. "Your kingdom come" is future. It is a request for something that is not now existing on earth. It is a request for the rule and reign of God and of His kingdom. The believer is to pray "your kingdom come."

For I tell you that unless your righteousness surpasses, that of the Pharisees, and the teachers of the law, you will certainly not enter the kingdom of heaven. (Mt. 5:20)

"Then the King will say to those on his right, 'Come, you who are blessed by my Father; take your inheritance, the kingdom prepared for you since the creation of the world. (Mt. 25:34)

Strengthening the disciples and encouraging them to remain true to the faith. "We must go through many hardships to enter the kingdom of God," they said. (Acts 14:22)

Listen, my dear brothers: Has not God chosen those who are poor in the eyes of the world to be rich in faith and to inherit the kingdom he promised those who love him? (James 2:5)

He who testifies to these things says, "Yes, I am coming soon." Amen. Come, Lord Jesus. (Rev 22:20)

Thought 4. God's kingdom *is* available. God's kingdom is desperately needed on earth right now. So much just eats and gnaws away at man—so much rebellion, wickedness, evil, enmity, bitterness, hatred, murder, injustice, deprivation, and hunger. God's rule and reign are needed now. The believer needs to see the urgency to pray and to pray consistently "Your kingdom come," and to live as if God's kingdom had already come.

DEEPER STUDY #6

(6:10) *God, Will of:* "Your will be done" says three critical things to God.

1. That we will work to please God in all we do. We will do our part to see that God's will is done on earth.
2. That God can do with us as He pleases. No matter what He chooses for us, we put ourselves at His disposal; for His use—even if it requires the sacrifice of all we are, and have.
3. That we will not be displeased with what God does. We may not understand; it may not make sense; there may be question after question; but we know that God's will is best, and He will work all things out for good.

Thought 1. "Your will be done on earth, as it is in heaven" is the second request to be prayed. The believer is to pray like this:

⇨ "Father, your will be done: your will and your will alone. There is no will but your will. Let it be done right here on earth...."

Thought 2. There are four wills that struggle for man's obedience.
1) Man's own will (Rom. 12:1-2; cp. Rom. 7:15f, Gal. 5:17).
2) Other men's wills (1 Pet. 4:2).

3) Satan's will (Jn. 8:44).
4) God's will (Eph. 5:15-17, esp. vs. 17; Ph. 2:13; 1 Jn. 2:17).

Thought 3. Note three significant lessons.

1) Many call God King, but they do not honor Him as a King. They do not do His will. Their profession is false, and tragically it creates an image of a false and meaningless King to the world.

2) We *must know God's will* if God's will is to be done. This requires study: "Do your best to present yourself to God as one approved" (2 Tim. 2:15). The only way God's will can be done is for us to study His Word and ask for the wisdom and strength to apply it to our lives (2 Tim. 3:16).

3) We are to ask for God's will to be done *on earth.* The earth is the place where God's will is so desperately needed. It is the place...
 • where there is so much sin and corruption
 • where there is so much suffering and pain
 • where there is so much struggling and death.
 • where the believer faces his trials

"I am the Lord's servant," Mary answered. "May it be to me as you have said." Then the angel left her. (Luke 1:38)

Do not offer the parts of your body to sin, as instruments of wickedness, but rather offer yourselves to God, as those who have been brought from death to life; and offer the parts of your body to him as instruments of righteousness. (Rom. 6:13)

Submit yourselves, then, to God. Resist the devil, and he will flee from you. (James 4:7)

I desire to do your will, O my God; your law is within my heart." (Psa. 40:8)

Teach me to do your will, for you are my God; may your good Spirit lead me on level ground. (Psa. 143:10).

4) "Your will be done on earth as it is in heaven." The believer is praying for *heaven (heaven's rule) to come to earth.* He is making a commitment to make earth more like heaven.
   a) By yielding himself "to God, as those who have been brought from death to life...." (Rom. 6:13).
   b) By going and teaching "all nations... to obey everything I [Christ] have commanded you" (Mt. 28:19-20).

DEEPER STUDY #7

(6:11) *Bread:* bread is the basic necessity of life, the symbol of all that is necessary for survival and for a full life. There is much meaning in this simple request.

1. "Give <u>us</u>...<u>our</u> bread." The words *our* and *us* overcome selfishness and show concern for others. Any person who goes to bed hungry should be of concern to the believer.
2. "<u>Today.</u>" This eliminates worry and anxiety about tomorrow and the distant future. It also teaches and helps us to trust God day by day. "The righteous will live by faith...." day by day.
3. "Our <u>daily</u> bread." Every believer has a portion of daily bread which is his. He does not ask for someone else's bread but for his own. He seeks and works for his own bread; he does not think of stealing or of eating from another man's table (2 Th. 3:10).
4. "Give us ... <u>bread.</u>" We ask for the necessities, not

the desserts of this world.

5. "<u>Give us</u> ... bread." The believer confesses his inadequacy and dependency upon God. He is dependent upon God even for the basics of life.

6. "Give ... today our <u>daily bread</u>." This teaches the believer to come to God daily in prayer and trust Him to meet his needs.

Thought 1. "Give us today our daily bread" is the third request to be prayed. The believer should pray like this:

⇨ "Father give us our bread today, spiritually as well as physically. Feed our souls and our bodies. Make this a glorious day in You. And, O God, the world is starving for You, and many are starving from hunger...."

Thought 2. God cares for man and his welfare.

1) He cares for man's physical well-being (Mt. 6:11; Mt. 6:25-34).

So do not worry, saying, 'What shall we eat?' or 'What shall we drink?' or 'What shall we wear?' (Mt. 6:31)

For the pagans run after all these things, and your heavenly Father knows that you need them. (Mt. 6:32)

But seek first his kingdom and his righteousness, and all these things will be given to you as well. (Mt. 6:33).

2) He cares for man's mental and emotional well-being.

For God did not give us a spirit of timidity, but a spirit of power, of love and of self-discipline. (2 Tim. 1:7)

Finally, brothers, whatever is true, whatever is noble, whatever is right, whatever is, pure, whatever is lovely, whatever is admirable—if anything is excellent or praiseworthy—think about such things. (Phil. 4:8)

And the God of all grace, who called you to his eternal glory in Christ, after you have suffered a little while, will himself restore you and make you strong, firm and steadfast. (1 Pet. 5:10)

3) He cares for man's spiritual well-being.

Don't you know that you yourselves are God's temple and that God's Spirit lives in you? (1 Cor. 3:16)

If anyone destroys God's temple, God will destroy him; for God's temple is sacred, and you are that temple. (1 Cor. 3:17)

Do you not know that your body is a temple of the Holy Spirit, who is in you, whom you have received from God? You are not your own; (1 Cor. 6:19)

You were bought at a price. Therefore honor God with your body. (1 Cor. 6:20)

Thought 3. God cares for the human body. Several things show this.

1) He said to ask for the necessities of life, daily (Mt. 6:11).
2) He sent His only Son into the world in a human body.
3) He raised up Christ in His body, a resurrected body.
4) He promises to give a new resurrected body to the believer. The believer will dwell in "the resurrected body" forever.
5) He has chosen the believer's body to be "a temple of the Holy Spirit" (1 Cor. 6:19-20).

Thought 4. This simple request is a great lesson for both the rich and the poor.

1) The rich man feels self-sufficient, as though what he possesses came from his own hands. Therefore, he thinks, "Who is the Lord?"

2) The poor man has nothing and is often forced to steal. Thus, he raises his fist in anger and curses God for his state of life.

> *Keep falsehood and lies far from me; give me neither poverty nor riches, but give me only my daily bread. (Prov. 30:8)*

> *Otherwise, I may have too much and disown you and say, 'Who is the LORD?' Or I may become poor and steal, and so dishonor the name of my God. (Prov. 30:9)*

The believer is to trust God for the necessities of life and praise God for what he receives. He has learned to be "content in any and every situation" (Ph. 4:11; cp. 4:12-13).

DEEPER STUDY #8

(6:12) *Forgiveness, Spiritual:* the word "debts" (opheilema) means dues, duties, that which is owed, that which is legally due. In relation to sin, it means a failure to pay one's debts, one's dues; a failure to do one's duty; to keep one's responsibilities.

God has given man certain responsibilities, certain things to do and not to do. Every man has failed at some point to do what he should. Certainly no man would ever claim he has fulfilled his duty perfectly—without any failure, without any shortcoming. Sin is universal. Everyone fails in his duty at some point to some degree. Everyone needs to pray "forgive us our debts, as we also have forgiven our debtors."

This prayer is asking God to do three things.
1. To forgive *the debt of sin*. One has failed God in his duty; therefore, he needs God to forgive his debt.
2. To forgive *the debt of guilt or punishment*. One who has failed to pay his debts is guilty; therefore, he is to pay the consequences; he is to be punished. This is the reason he must pray "Father, forgive my debts...."
3. To forgive *his debts just as he has forgiven* his debtors. This is asking God to forgive one exactly as he forgives others. If one forgives, God forgives. If one does not forgive, God does not forgive. Therefore, any person who holds anything against another person is not forgiven his sins, no matter what he may think or has been told by another person. (Cp. Mt. 6:14-15).

Thought 1. "Forgive us our debts, as we also have forgiven our debtors" is the fourth request to be prayed. The believer should pray:
1) "Father, forgive me—have mercy upon me, the sinner, the nothing. O' God, You are all—have mercy...."
2) "Father, forgive others—all others, I hold nothing within. O' God, if there is anything within my heart against anyone, help me to forgive...."

Thought 2. In seeking forgiveness we have a duty both to God and to man.
1) Our duty to God is to ask forgiveness when we fail to do His will.

If we confess our sins, he is faithful and just and will forgive us our sins and purify us from all unrighteousness. (1 John 1:9)

Let the wicked forsake his way and the evil man his thoughts. Let him turn to the LORD, and he will have mercy on him, and to our God, for he will freely pardon. (Isa. 55:7)

I will cleanse them from all the sin they have committed against me and will forgive all their sins of rebellion against me. (Jer. 33:8)

2) Our duty to man is to forgive his sins against us.

And when you stand praying, if you hold anything against anyone, forgive him, so that your Father in heaven may forgive you your sins. (Mark 11:25)

If he sins against you seven times in a day, and seven times comes back to you and says, 'I repent,' forgive him. (Lk. 17:4)

Be kind and compassionate to one another, forgiving each other, just as in Christ God forgave you. (Eph. 4:32)

Bear with each other and forgive whatever grievances you may have against one another. Forgive as the Lord forgave you. (Col. 3:13)

If we wish to be forgiven ourselves, both duties have to be performed. We must forgive those who sin against us (Mt. 6:12), and, we must ask forgiveness for our sins (1 Jn. 1:9).

Thought 3. There are those who do us much evil. In this world many say and do all manner of evil against us. Bad news and evil purposes run wild, and it is not always *outside* the church, nor *outside* the family. Sometimes terrible evil is committed by word and act both within the church and within a person's family (Eph. 4:30-32; cp. Mt.10:21; Mk. 13:12-13). Christ says we must not react nor be harsh toward those who sin severely against us, but we must forgive. We must forgive if we wish to be forgiven.

⇨ Some strike us (Mt. 5:39).

⇨ Some hate us (Mt. 5:44).

⇨ Some compel us against our will (Mt. 5:41).

⇨ Some sue us (Mt. 5:40).

⇨ Some curse us (Mt. 5:44).

⇨ Some persecute us (Mt. 5:44).

⇨ Some spread rumors about us (Mt. 5:11).

Thought 4. There are four things a believer must do when sinned against.

1) The believer must understand (Pr. 11:12; 15:21; 17:27-28; cp. Eph. 1:8). There is always a reason why a person sins against a believer. Too often we forget this.

   a. A person may be mistreated by someone who is close to him. He may be withdrawn from, neglected, and ignored. Therefore, he may react against a believer, and the reaction may range from self-pity to bitterness and hostility.

   b. A person may be tired, aggravated, and worried. Therefore, he may become too direct or cutting or harsh toward the believer.

   c . A person may be of a shy nature or sense inferiority; therefore, he may act unfriendly and unconcerned toward the believer.

   d. A person may have rumor and gossip and wild imaginations shared with him, especially by a person who has been hurt; he may be lied to and misinformed. Therefore, he may act suspicious and have nothing to do with the believer.

e. A person may have a great need for attention and for emotional support. Therefore, the person may imagine, exaggerate, blame, or accuse a believer in order to rally the support of friends and to gain the attention needed.

2) The believer must forbear (Eph. 4:2; Col. 3:13).
3) The believer must forgive (Eph. 4:31-32).
4) The believer must forget, that is, not harbor the wrong done to him (Ph. 3:13; cp. 2 Cor. 10:5).

Thought 5. Note four additional lessons that need to be noted.

1) An unforgiving spirit causes pain and hurt and tragedy—both to oneself and others. It can ruin lives, especially the lives of those closest and dearest to oneself.
2) We can curse ourselves by praying the Lord's prayer. We are in trouble when praying the Lord's prayer if we are angry and do not forgive those who sin against us: "Father... forgive us... <u>as we also have forgiven</u> our debtors." We pronounce the very same judgment upon ourselves that we hold for others.
3) Forgiveness is conditional. The reason is simply explained. We have sinned against God, and others have sinned against us. If we want God to forgive us, we must forgive those who have sinned against us. How can we expect God to forgive us if we do not forgive those who have sinned against us? We can expect no better treatment than we give.
4) Forgiving others is evidence that God has forgiven our sins.

DEEPER STUDY #9

(6:13) *Temptation—Deliverance:* God does not lead a man to sin; He tempts no man (Jas. 1:13). What Christ is saying is two things.

1. Pray—pray that God will keep you from the awful pull of temptation. The believer is to have a sense of his personal weakness against temptation.
2. Pray—pray that God will deliver you from evil. The Greek says "from the evil one," that is, Satan. The request is for God to rescue, preserve, and guard us. He, the evil one, is so deceptive and powerful; he is as powerful as a roaring lion (1 Pet. 5:8).

The plea and the cry is for God to deliver us from (1) temptation and (2) from the evil one. (Cp. Rom. 8:31, I Jn. 4:4; cp. I Cor. 10:13. Also see outlines—Jas. 4:7-10; see note I and DEEPER STUDY# 1 – Lk. 4:1-2.)

Thought 1. "Lead us not into temptation, but deliver us from the evil one" is the fifth request to be prayed. The believer should pray like this:

⇨ "Father, lead us not into temptation. Temptation comes so often; its pull is so strong. We get in the way so much. We seek our own way and react at every turn. O' God do not leave us to ourselves....

⇨ "And, dear Father, deliver us from the evil one. He is the master of deceit and paints such a beautiful picture. If you leave us to ourselves, we will fall. And, O' God, he is capable of being 'a roaring lion' seeking to devour us. Deliver us—rescue us—preserve us—guard us...."

Thought 2: Once we have been forgiven our sins (v. 12), we must ask God to keep us from sinning again. Two things are essential to keep us from sin: (1) deliverance from temptation (see DEEPER STUDY# 1—Lk.4:1-2), and (2) deliverance from "the evil one" (see DEEPER STUDY #1—Rev. 12:9).

Thought 3. This request is a necessity for every believer. Why? There are two reasons.
1) All believers are tempted and tempted often, not by strange things, but by things that are common to all. Temptations do come and will come to all—the same temptations (1 Cor. 10:13.)
2) No believer stands above falling:

> So, if you think you are standing firm, be careful that you don't fall! (1 Cor. 10:12)

Thought 4. Temptation is to be prayed against for two reasons.
1) Because sin causes God great hurt and pain (Ps. 15:4).
2) Because sin causes great trouble, guilt, and grief for both oneself and others (Lk. 19:41-44; cp. Mt. 23:37; Lk. 13:34).

Thought 5. The believer must have help in overcoming "the evil one." The *evil one* attacks (1) by deception (2 Cor. 11:3, 14-15; Rev. 12:9) and (2) by direct assault, seeking to devour (1 Pet. 5:8).

Thought 6: In dealing with "the evil one," the believer needs to remember two things.
1) "The one who is in you is greater than the one who is in the world" (1 Jn. 4:4).
2) "If God is for us, who can be against us?" (Rom. 8:31; cp. Rom. 8:31-39).

No temptation has seized you except what is common to man. And God is faithful; he will not let you be tempted beyond what you can bear. But when you are tempted, he will also provide a way out so that you can stand up under it. (1 Cor. 10:13)

Consider it pure joy, my brothers, whenever you face trials of many kinds. (James 1:2)

Because you know that the testing of your faith develops perseverance. (James 1:3)

Blessed is the man who perseveres under trial, because when he has stood the test, he will receive the crown of life that God has promised to those who love him. (James 1:12)

If this is so, then the Lord knows how to rescue godly men from trials and to hold the unrighteous for the day of judgment, while continuing their punishment. (2 Pet. 2:9)

To him who is able to keep you from falling and to present you before his glorious presence without fault and with great joy—(Jude 1:24)

To the only God our Savior be glory, majesty, power and authority, through Jesus Christ our Lord, before all ages, now and forevermore! Amen. (Jude 1:25)

Since you have kept my command to endure patiently, I will also keep you from the hour of trial that is going to come upon the whole world to test those who live on the earth. (Rev. 3:10)

3 (6:13) *Doxology—The kingdom and the power and the glory:* there is praise and commitment. These words are not in the best and oldest manuscripts of the Greek. Many scholars believe the doxology was added at a later date to be used in public worship. The NIV includes the following words in a footnote: "For yours is the kingdom and the power and the glory forever. Amen." Note: there is a similar doxology by David (1 Chr. 29:11). The point of the doxology is to stress that everything belongs to God.

1. He is *the Source* of the kingdom and the power and the glory.
2. He is *the Possessor* of the kingdom and the power and the glory.
3. He is *the Recipient* of the kingdom and the power and the glory.

The believer belongs to the kingdom and the power and the glory of God.

1. The believer belongs to God's kingdom: God has accepted the believer into the Kingdom of God and promises to transport him into the kingdom and its glory either at death or at the Lord's return.
2. The believer belongs to God's power: God has delivered him from sin and death and continues to deliver him daily.
3. The believer belongs to God's glory: God has done all for the believer that "in order that in the coming ages he might show the incomparable riches of his grace expressed in his kindness to us in Christ Jesus" (Eph. 2:7).

Thought 1. "For yours is the kingdom and the power and the glory forever. Amen" is the third major point to pray.

1) "Father, yours is the kingdom, the right to rule and reign ...."
2) "Yours is the power, the only power that can really rule and govern ...."
3) "Yours is the glory. O' God, all glory belongs to you ...."

Thought 2. Note three significant points.

1) "Yours is the kingdom" says two things.
   a) The right to rule and reign throughout the universe is God's. It belongs to no one else. The only perfect and eternal government is God's. The only government that possesses utopia, the very best of all, and that lasts forever is God's.
   b) The right to rule and reign belongs to no one else but God. Only God's government can bring utopia: love, joy, peace, and the very best of life.

"The God who made the world and everything in it is the Lord of heaven and earth and does not live in temples built by hands. (Acts 17:24)

And he is not served by human hands, as if he needed anything, because he himself gives all men life and breath and everything else. (Acts 17:25)

Acknowledge and take to heart this day that the LORD is God in heaven above and on the earth below. There is no other. (Deut. 4:39)

Wealth and honor come from you; you are the ruler of all things. In your hands are strength and power to exalt and give strength to all. (1 Chr. 29:12)

Let them know that you, whose name is the LORD—that you alone are the Most High over all the earth. (Psa. 83:18)

The LORD reigns, he is robed in majesty; the LORD is robed in majesty and is armed with strength. The world is firmly established; it cannot be moved. (Psa. 93:1)

And said: "Praise be to the name of God for ever and ever; wisdom and power are his. (Dan. 2:20)

He changes times and seasons; he sets up kings and deposes them. He gives wisdom to the wise and knowledge to the discerning. (Dan. 2:21)

All the peoples of the earth are regarded as nothing. He does as he pleases with the powers of heaven and the peoples of the earth. No one can hold back his hand or say to him: "What have you done?" (Dan. 4:35)

2) "Yours is the power" says two things.
   a) God alone has the power to create and sustain perfect government. He alone has the power to support and bring perfect government to man and his earth.
   b) God alone has the power to change men so that they can escape death and live forever within a perfect government. He alone has the power to stir men to live

in love, joy, and peace and to serve completely and unselfishly so that all may have the very best.

3) "Yours is the glory" says that God alone deserves all the honor and praise and glory. For what? For all. He is all in all.

Thought 3. The one subject that is to dominate prayer is "praising God." The fact that the Lord's prayer begins with praise (surrender, v.9) and ends with praise (v. 13b) shows this.

God does not *need* praise. He has the praise of multitudes of angels, but He *deserves* our praise.

⇨ God created us with the ability to praise Him. He must *want* our praise.

⇨ A genuine believer is always praising God's name before all.

DEEPER STUDY #10

(6:13) *Amen:* (This is not in the NIV Scripture; however it is being included as added information for the reader.) So be it; it is and shall be so. When spoken by God, "Amen" means it is and shall be so, unequivocally. When spoken by man it is a petition meaning, "Let it be." Here, in the Lord's Prayer, the word *Amen* is a word of commitment. When a man prays the Lord's prayer and closes by saying "Amen" (let it be), he is committing himself to do his part for the things which have been prayed.

MATTHEW 6:14-15

	O. The Basic Principle of Prayer (Part IV): Forgiveness[DS1,2] 6:14-15 (Mk. 11:25-26)
1 The promise: Forgive others & be forgiven	14 For if you forgive men when they sin against you, your heavenly Father will also forgive you.
2 The warning: Refuse to forgive others & be unforgiven	15 But if you do not forgive men their sins, your Father will not forgive your sins.

THE TEACHINGS OF THE MESSIAH TO
HIS DISCIPLES:
THE GREAT SERMON ON THE MOUNT,
5:1-7:29

O. THE BASIC PRINCIPLE OF PRAYER (PART IV): FORGIVENESS, 6:14-15

(6:14-15) *Introduction—Forgiveness:* note the first word, "for." This connects these verses to the Lord's Prayer. Immediately after closing the Lord's Prayer, Jesus explained why He had said that forgiveness is conditional (Mt. 6:12). This was a necessary explanation for two reasons.

1. The very idea that a person must forgive others in order for God to forgive him was totally new. It was a shocking concept, an eye-opener. It had to be explained.
2. The very idea of forgiveness is just what it says: it is forgiving. God knows that He cannot forgive an unforgiving heart. His nature of love and justice will not permit Him to indulge in sin and give license to the passions of a man's unforgiving spirit. He can forgive only where the mercy and tenderness of forgiveness are found. Therefore, Christ had to teach the basic principle of prayer—

forgiveness (Mt. 18:21-35; Mk. 11: 25-26; Lk. 6:37; 17:3-4; Eph. 4:32). (See DEEPER STUDY# 4— Mt. 26:28.)

1. The promise: forgive others and be forgiven (v. 14).
2. The warning: refuse to forgive others and be unforgiven (v. 15).

DEEPER STUDY #1

(6:14-15) *Forgiveness:* there are several prerequisites to forgiveness. For a man to be forgiven, he must do several things.

1. He must confess his sins (1 Jn. 1:9; cp. 1 Jn. 1:8-10).
2. He must have faith in God: a belief that God will actually forgive (Heb. 11:6)
3. He must repent (turn away from and forsake his sins) and turn to God in a renewed commitment (see note—Acts 3:19; note 7 and DEEPER STUDY #1 –17:29-30; note—Lk. 17:3-4).
4. He must forgive those who have wronged him (Mt. 6:14-15). Hard feelings or anger against a person is sin. It is evidence that a person has not truly turned from his sins and that he is *not really* sincere in seeking forgiveness.

DEEPER STUDY #2

(6:14-15) *Forgiveness:* there are four different attitudes toward forgiveness.

1. The attitude of the agnostic or doubter. God may be; He may not be. Therefore forgiveness from God is immaterial. It does not matter. All that matters is for

men to forgive each other and relate properly.
Forgiveness from an invisible, personal God is a far-
fetched idea.

2. The attitude of the guilt or conscience-stricken person.
   This is a person who knows little, if anything, about
   a personal God, yet he is deeply conscious of guilt
   and the need for forgiveness. He prays for forgiveness
   over and over, but he never comes to know forgiveness.

3. The attitude of the social religionist. This is a person
   who is sometimes mentally aware of the need for
   forgiveness; therefore, he makes an occasional
   confession. He feels forgiven, arises and goes about
   his affairs with no more thought about the matter. The
   problem with this is that it is a false forgiveness, a
   mental forgiveness. The person views God as a *patsy*
   — *grandfather* who allows a person to live like he
   wishes as long as he occasionally confesses. He ignores
   and denies the righteousness and justice of a loving
   God.

4. The attitude of the mature believer. This is a believer
   who truly knows his own sinful self and his great need
   for God's forgiveness. Therefore, he lives in a spirit
   of confession and repentance, by which he comes to
   know God's forgiveness and the assurance of it (see
   note—Rom. 8:2-4).

1 (6:14) **Forgiveness of Others:** there is the promise
to forgive and thereby to be forgiven. The word
"trespass" (paraptoma) means to stumble; to fall; to
slip; to blunder; to deviate from righteousness and
truth. Note three things.

1. Christ takes for granted that we know that we
   need forgiveness. This is seen in His words, "your
   heavenly Father will also <u>forgive</u> you." We are

sinners; we have transgressed God's law and we need forgiveness. Even the most mature among us fails to keep God's law perfectly. We all stumble, fall, blunder, and slip; and we do it much too often.

a. We are seldom doing to the fullest degree what we should do. We come short.

b. We are always *crossing over* from the path we should be following. We deviate over into *the forbidden* area. Thus, we desperately need forgiveness. God promises that He will forgive our sins if we will do one simple thing: forgive men their sins.

2. The greatest thing in all the world is to be forgiven our sins: to be absolved and released from all guilt and condemnation, to be accepted and restored by God and assured of seeing Christ face to face. Forgiveness of sins means that we are freed: set at liberty in this life to live abundantly, and set at liberty in the next life to live eternally in perfection.

3. The only way we can be forgiven our sins is to forgive others their sins. Christ makes the promise: "Forgive men their sins [and] your heavenly Father will also forgive you." Forgiving men their sins means several very practical things.

⇨ We are not judgmental or censorious.

⇨ We do not become bitter or hostile.

⇨ We do not plan to take revenge.

⇨ We do not hold hard feelings against another person.

⇨ We do not talk about, gossip, or join in rumor; on the contrary, we correct the rumor.

⇨ We do not rejoice in trouble and trials that fall upon another person.

⇨ We love and pray for the person.

Thought 1. Note two facts.

1) Bad feelings against another person is sin. It is holding sin within our heart. Forgiving a person who has done us evil is proof that we wish to have a clean heart. We really wish God to forgive us.

2) Forgiving men their sins does not refer only to the sins against us, but all sins.

Blessed are the merciful, for they will be shown mercy. (Mt. 5:7)

And when you stand praying, if you hold anything against anyone, forgive him, so that your Father in heaven may forgive you your sins." (Mark 11:25)

Forgive us our sins, for we also forgive everyone who sins against us. And lead us not into temptation. (Luke 11:4)

If he sins against you seven times in a day, and seven times comes back to you and says, 'I repent,' forgive him. (Luke 17:4)

Bear with each other and forgive whatever grievances you may have against one another. Forgive as the Lord forgave you. (Col. 3:13)

2 (15) **Forgiveness of Others:** there is the warning—refuse to forgive and be unforgiven. The believer who prays for forgiveness and holds feelings against another person is hypocritical. He is asking God to do something he himself is unwilling to do. He is asking God to forgive his sins when he himself is unwilling to forgive the sins of others. Bad feelings against a person are clear proof that a person is not right with God.

1.   Bad feelings show that a person does not know the true nature of man nor of God. He does not know the true exalted perfection of God nor the real depth of man's sinful nature—how far short he is of perfect righteousness.

2.   Bad feelings show that a person walks and lives in self-righteousness (that is, that he thinks that he is acceptable to God by deeds of righteousness) He feels better than others, and judges himself able to talk about and look askance at the sins of others.

3.   Bad feelings show that a person has not taken the steps he must take in order to be forgiven his own sins (see DEEPER STUDY #1, 2—Mt. 6:14-15).

4.   Bad feelings show that a person is living by the standards of society and not by God's Word. God's Word is clear: "there is no one who does good, not even one" (Rom. 3:12; cp. Mt. 19:17). Therefore, we are to help and love one another, and care and restore one another when we stumble, slip, fall, blunder, and deviate.

As it is written: "There is no one righteous, not even one; (Rom. 3:10; cp. Rom. 3:9-19)

For all have sinned and fall short of the glory of God, (Rom. 3:23)

Get rid of all bitterness, rage and anger, brawling and slander, along with every form of malice. Be kind and compassionate to one another, forgiving each other, just as in Christ God forgave you. (Eph. 4:31-32)

Brothers, if someone is caught in a sin, you who are spiritual should restore him gently. But watch yourself, or you also may be tempted. Carry each other's burdens, and in this way you will fulfill the law of Christ. If anyone thinks he is something when he is nothing, he deceives himself. (Gal. 6:1-3)

Christ is explicitly clear in His warning about forgiving others.

Be merciful, just as your Father is merciful. Do not judge, and you will not be judged. Do not condemn, and you will not be condemned. Forgive, and you will be forgiven. (Luke 6:36-37)

The warning is severe when the opposite statement is seen: "Do not judge, and you will not be judged. Do not condemn, and you will not be condemned. Forgive, and you will be forgiven" (cp. Lk. 6:36-37).

Thought 1. Note three significant lessons in this point.
1) The man who holds bad feelings against others has not looked at himself and his own sins. He does not know himself, not his real self, not the inner selfishness and motives that plague the depravity of man.

2) Feelings against others cause inward disturbance. They eat away at a person's mind and emotions to varying degrees. Deep feelings against others can cause deep emotional and mental problems as well as serious physical problems.

3) Three things are necessary for God to hear our prayer for forgiveness of sins. (1) Lifting up holy hands, (2) being without wrath, and (3) not doubting.

I want men everywhere to lift up holy hands in prayer, without anger or disputing. (1 Tim. 2:8)

Thought 2. The answer to peace is Christ Jesus. "He Himself is our peace"—the only possible peace between two persons (see outline and notes— Eph. 2:14-18. Review the Scriptures below verse by verse in light of the following facts.)

1) He can make both one (Eph. 2:14).
2) He can break down the wall between both (Eph. 2:14).
3) He can abolish the enmity—in His own flesh (Eph. 2:15).
4) He can make the two into one new man (Eph. 2:15).
5) He can reconcile both to God—in one body— by the cross (Eph. 2:15).
6) He can give peace to both and bring peace between both (Eph. 2:17).
7) He can give both access to God the Father (Eph. 2:18).

MATTHEW 6:16-18

<table>
<tr><td></td><td>P. The Right Motive for Fasting, 6:16-18</td></tr>
<tr><td>

1 The wrong way to fast
  a. Fasting as a hypocrite
  b. Fasting for recognition

  c. Reward: To receive
    only human
    recognition & esteem

2 The right way to fast[DS1,2]
  a. Fasting as a duty
  b. Fasting without notice
  c. Fasting to God alone

  d. Reward: God shall
    reward openly

</td><td>

16 "When you fast, do not look somber as the hypocrites do, for they disfigure their faces to show men they are fasting. I tell you the truth, they have received their reward in full.
17 But when you fast, put oil on your head and wash your face,
18 So that it will not be obvious to men that you are fasting, but only to your Father, who is unseen; and your Father, who sees what is done in secret, will reward you.

</td></tr>
</table>

THE TEACHINGS OF THE MESSIAH TO
HIS DISCIPLES:
THE GREAT SERMON ON THE MOUNT,
5:1-7:29

P. THE RIGHT MOTIVE FOR FASTING, 6:16-18

(6:16-18) *Introduction—Fasting:* fasting means to abstain from food for some religious or spiritual purpose. A study of the fasting practiced by Jesus and by the great leaders of the Bible reveals what God means by fasting. Very simply, fasting means being so consumed with a matter that it becomes more important than food. Therefore, the believer sets food aside *in order to concentrate on seeking God about the matter.* Biblical fasting means more than just abstaining from food; it means to abstain from food in order to concentrate upon God and His answer to a particular matter. Biblical fasting involves prayer, intense supplication before God. Note the words "when you fast" (v.16, 17). Jesus assumed believers fasted; He expected them to fast. He fasted and He taught fasting (Mt. 4:2), and the early believers fasted (Mt. 17:21; Lk. 2:37; Acts 10:30; 13:3; 14:23; 1 Cor. 7:5; 2 Cor. 6:5; 11:27). Yet so few have continued such intense seeking of the Lord: so few fast, truly fast.

The benefits of fasting are enormous, but there are also dangers. We can fast for the wrong reasons. This is the point of the present passage. Christ counsels us on the wrong and the right motives for fasting.

1. The wrong way to fast (v. 16).
2. The right way to fast (v. 17-18).

1 (6:16) *Fasting:* the wrong way to fast.

1. Fasting as a hypocrite is wrong. Being hypocritical is a real danger when fasting. There are four reasons men fast, and all but one are false and hypocritical.
   a. Men fast to gain a sense of God's approval and of self-approval.
   b. Men fast to fulfill a religious act.
   c. Men fast to gain religious recognition.
   d. Men fast to genuinely meet God for some special purpose.

Thought 1. Fasting is not condemned by Christ. Fasting for any purpose other than to meet God is condemned: when you fast, fast "only to your Father" (v. 18).

"So when you give to the needy, do not announce it with trumpets, as the hypocrites do in the synagogues and on the streets, to be honored by men. I tell you the truth, they have received their reward in full. (Mt. 6:2)

"These people honor me with their lips, but their hearts are far from me. (Mt. 15:8)

I fast twice a week and give a tenth of all I get. (Luke 18:12)

Having a form of godliness but denying its power. Have nothing to do with them. (2 Tim. 3:5)

The Lord says: "These people come near to me with their mouth and honor me with their lips, but their hearts are far from me. Their worship of me is made up only of rules taught by men. (Isa. 29:13)

For I desire mercy, not sacrifice, and acknowledgment of God rather than burnt offerings. (Hosea 6:6)

2. Fasting for recognition is wrong. It poses several serious dangers that must be guarded against with all diligence.
    a. The danger of feeling superspiritual. Few believers follow a true fast. Therefore when they really fast, they have to guard against a sense of superspirituality and pride.
    b. The danger of overconfidence. The believer's confidence is to be in God, not in self. After a genuine fast a believer usually feels spiritually confident, ready to go forth. He must go forth depending upon the strength of Christ and not upon his own energy and effort.
    c. The danger of sharing one's fasting experience. The believer has usually learned so much from being in God's presence that he is anxious to share it, especially with those closest to him.

The best advice is to hush: share nothing, not even with one's dearest friend.

d. The danger of changing one's appearance, and the way one acts and behaves. Any change whatsoever from one's normal behavior and routine attracts attention and ruins the whole benefit of the fast. As Christ says, "they disfigure their faces" (act superspiritual) (v. 16).

"Everything they do is done for men to see: They make their phylacteries wide and the tassels on their garments long; (Mt. 23:5)

"Woe to you, teachers of the law and Pharisees, you hypocrites! You are like whitewashed tombs, which look beautiful on the outside but on the inside are full of dead men's bones and everything unclean. (Mt. 23:27)

Stop judging by mere appearances, and make a right judgment." (John 7:24)

You are looking only on the surface of things. If anyone is confident that he belongs to Christ, he should consider again that we belong to Christ just as much as he. (2 Cor. 10:7)

3. Fasting the wrong way has its reward. A person will receive human recognition and esteem, but the recognition of men is all he will ever receive.

Thought 1. Some gain the control and discipline of their bodies through fasting, but they ruin themselves and their ministry through pride. They lose their reward.

For, "All men are like grass, and all their glory is like the flowers of the field; the grass withers and the flowers fall, (1 Pet. 1:24)

But man, despite his riches, does not endure; he is like the beasts that perish. (Psa. 49:12)

For he will take nothing with him when he dies, his splendor will not descend with him. (Psa. 49:17)

Therefore the grave enlarges its appetite and opens its mouth without limit; into it will descend their nobles and masses with all their brawlers and revelers. (Isa. 5:14)

The more the priests increased, the more they sinned against me; they exchanged their Glory for something disgraceful. (Hosea 4:7)

2 (17-18) **Fasting:** the right way to fast. As stated in the introduction, fasting means being so consumed with a matter that it becomes more important than food. Therefore, the believer sets food aside *in order to concentrate on seeking* God about the matter. Biblical fasting means more than just abstaining from food; it means to abstain from food in order to concentrate upon God and His answer to a particular matter. Biblical fasting involves prayer, intense supplication before God.

1. Fasting is a duty. Every believer is expected to fast. Christ said "When you fast." He expects us to fast.
    ⇨ Jesus Himself fasted.

After fasting forty days and forty nights, he was hungry. (Mt. 4:2)

⇨ The apostles were to fast.

Jesus answered, "How can the guests of the bridegroom mourn while he is with them? The time will come when the bridegroom will be taken from them; then they will fast." (Mt. 9:15; cp. Mk. 2:20; Lk. 5:35)

⇨ Anna fasted.

And then was a widow until she was eighty-four. She never left the temple but worshiped night and day, fasting and praying. (Luke 2:37)

⇨ Cornelius fasted.

Cornelius answered: "Four days ago I was in my house praying at this hour, at three in the· afternoon. Suddenly a man in shining clothes stood before me (Acts 10:30)

⇨ Church leaders fasted.

While they were worshiping the Lord and fasting, the Holy Spirit said, "Set apart for me Barnabas and Saul for the work to which I have called them." (Acts 13:2)

Paul and Barnabas appointed elders for them in each church and, with prayer and fasting, committed them to the Lord, in whom they had put their trust. (Acts 14:23)

⇨ Husbands and wives are expected to fast.

Do not deprive each other except by mutual consent and for a time, so that you may devote yourselves to prayer. Then come together again so that Satan will not tempt you because of your lack of self-control. (1 Cor. 7:5)

⇨ Paul fasted often.

In beatings, imprisonments and riots; in hard work, sleepless nights and hunger; (2 Cor. 6:5)

I have labored and toiled and have often gone without sleep; I have known hunger and thirst and have often gone without food; I have been cold and naked. (2 Cor. 11:27)

2. Fasting is to be done without notice. The believer is to fast before God, not before men. There is to be no change in appearance or behavior to indicate that he is fasting. Think about it. Why should there be? Why should anyone know that a person is seeking God in a very special way? The matter is God's affair, not man's affair. It is between the person and God, not the person and other people.

Thought 1. What is fasting? It is not to be "obvious to men ... but only to your Father" (v. 18). It is to come into God's presence for a very, very special session of prayer.

3. Fasting is to be to God alone. The believer is to fast to God alone. God is the object of his fast. He needs to meet God in a very, very special

way. In meeting God all alone, the believer is demonstrating his dependency upon God and His provision. (See note—Mt.6:16-18.)

Thought 1. A religionist fasts before men. A genuine believer fasts before God.

Thought 2. God does not say when nor how often we should fast, but He does tell us how to fast. We must take every precaution to fast exactly as He says: before God, in secret, without any ostentation or show whatsoever. No one is to see or know.

4. Fasting the right way has its reward: God shall reward us openly. How much greater is His reward than the recognition of men! God's acceptance and eternal reward is enough for genuine believers.

But when you give to the needy, do not let your left hand know what your right hand is doing, so that your giving may be in secret. Then your Father, who sees what is done in secret, will reward you. (Mt. 6:34)

For we must all appear before the judgment seat of Christ, that each one may receive what is due him for the things done while in the body, whether good or bad. (2 Cor. 5:10)

Watch out that you do not lose what you have worked for, but that you may be rewarded fully. (2 John 1:8)

"Behold, I am coming soon! My reward is with me, and I will give to everyone according to what he has done. (Rev. 22:12)

The fear of the LORD is pure, enduring forever. The ordinances of the LORD are sure and altogether righteous .... By them is your servant warned; in keeping them there is great reward. (Psa. 19:9, 11)

Then men will say, "Surely the righteous still are rewarded; surely there is a God who judges the earth." (Psa. 58:11)

See, the Sovereign LORD comes with power, and his arm rules for him. See, his reward is with him, and his recompense accompanies him. (Isa. 40:10)

The LORD has made proclamation to the ends of the earth: "Say to the Daughter of Zion, 'See, your Savior comes! See, his reward is with him, and his recompense accompanies him.'" (Isa. 62:11)

"I the LORD search the heart and examine the mind, to reward a man according to his conduct, according to what his deeds deserve." (Jer. 17:10)

Can anyone hide in secret places so that I cannot see him?" declares the LORD. "Do not I fill heaven and earth?" declares the LORD. (Jer. 23:24)

DEEPER STUDY #1

(6:17-18) *Fasting:* there are at least four times when the believer should fast.

1. There are times when the believer feels a special pull, an urge, a call within his heart to get alone with God. This is God's Spirit moving within his heart. When this happens, nothing—not food, not responsibility—should keep him from getting all alone with God. He should fast as soon as possible.
2. There are times when special needs arise. The needs may concern the believer's own life or the life of friends, society, the world, or some ministry or mission. Again, nothing should keep the believer from spending a very special time in God's presence when facing such dire needs.
3. There are times when the believer needs to humble his soul before God. At such times he learns not only humility but dependence upon God (Ps. 35:13).
4. There are times when the believer needs a very special power from God. The Lord promised such power if the believer prayed and fasted (Mt. 17:21; Mk. 9:29).

DEEPER STUDY #2

(6:17-18) *Fasting:* Why are believers to fast? There are excellent benefits to fasting, and God wants His people to reap these benefits.

1. Fasting keeps the believer in the presence of God. He is fasting in order to seek God's presence for a very special purpose; he remains in God's presence until he feels God has or is going to meet his need.

2. Fasting humbles the believer's soul before God. It says that God is the most important thing in all the world to him (Ps. 35:13).

3. Fasting teaches the believer his dependency upon God. He is seeking God, and in so doing he is demonstrating his conviction that he is dependent upon God.

4. Fasting demonstrates to God (by action) a real seriousness. It shows by act that the matter being considered is a priority.

5. Fasting teaches the believer to control and discipline his life. He does without in order to gain a greater substance.

6. Fasting keeps the believer from being enslaved by habit. He lays aside all substances; in so doing, he breaks the hold of anything that might have him chained.

7. Fasting helps the believer to stay physically fit. It helps keep him from becoming overweight and soft.

MATTHEW 6:19-24

1 A contrast: About two kinds of riches
  a. Earthly riches
    1) Are not to be laid up
    2) Are destroyed[DS1]
    3) Are insecure
  b. Heavenly riches
    1) Are to be laid up
    2) Are indestructible
    3) Are secure

2 A warning: About two kinds of hearts
  a. A good heart: Like a good eye
    1) Focuses & sees
    2) Focuses on heaven (v. 20)
  b. A bad heart: Like a bad eye
    1) Blind and dark
    2) Focuses on the earth (v. 19)

3 A choice: About two kinds of Masters
  a. Either hate or love
  b. Either cleave or despise
  c. The choice: Serve God or material things[DS2]

Q. The Warning About Wealth & Materialism, 6:19-24

19 "Do not store up for yourselves treasures on earth, where moth and rust destroy, and where thieves break in and steal.
20 But store up for yourselves treasures in heaven, where moth and rust do not destroy, and where thieves do not break in and steal.
21 For where your treasure is, there your heart will be also.
22 "The eye is the lamp of the body. If your eyes are good, your whole body will be full of light.
23 But if your eyes are bad, your whole body will be full of darkness. If then the light within you is darkness, how great is that darkness!
24 "No one can serve two masters. Either he will hate the one and love the other, or he will be devoted to the one and despise the other. You cannot serve both God and Money.

The Teachings of the Messiah to
His Disciples:
The Great Sermon on the Mount,
5:1-7:29

Q. The Warning About Wealth and Materialism, 6:19-24

(6:19-24) **Introduction:** Where are our thoughts? What do we think about? Are our thoughts on earth or on heaven? Is our mind on earthly things or on God? What are we seeking, the things of the earth or the things of heaven? Where is our heart, focused on earth or focused on heaven? The concern of Christ in this passage is money, possessions, and material things. His concern is that we guard against centering our lives around houses, furnishings, cars, lands, buildings, stocks—all the things that make up security and wealth on this earth. The reason is simply understood: nothing on this earth is secure and lasting. It is aging, decaying, and wasting away. It is all corruptible and temporal. What Christ wants is for us to center our lives around Him and heaven, for everything about Himself and heaven is life and security. It is all permanent and eternal. To stir our thinking He gives us a lesson on wealth and materialism. (Also see outline and DEEPER STUDY #3—Mt. 13:7, 22.)

1. A contrast: about two kinds of riches (v. 19-20).
2. A warning: about two kinds of hearts (v. 21-23).
3. A choice: about two kinds of masters (v. 24).

1 (6:19-20) *Materialism—Wealth:* Christ gives a contrast about two kinds of riches.

1. There are earthly riches. There are things on earth that men desire. Christ calls these earthly riches and treasures. Earthly riches would be such things as clothes, cars, jewelry, toys, houses, buildings, furnishings, pleasure, fame, power, profession, property, money—anything that dominates a person's life and holds it fast to this earth.

A treasure is that which has value and is worth something to someone. Men take things and ascribe value to them: it may be stones (diamonds); or rocks and dust (gold); or money (paper and metal); or land (property); or wood, metal, dirt, chemical, and fabric (buildings); or influence (power); or the attention of people (fame).

Christ says three things about earthly riches that are of critical importance to both the believer and the unbeliever.

   a. Do not store up for yourselves earthly riches (material possessions). Christ says that a person is not to focus his life on earthly things, not to set his eyes and mind and energy and effort on such passing treasures.

Thought 1. Riches do exist. And their *locality is* clearly stated. There is wealth both on *earth* and in *heaven*.

Thought 2. It is easier to covet earthly things than heavenly things for four reasons.
1) They are seen and can be handled.
2) They are sought by most people, and other people influence us. A person is either worldly minded or heavenly minded (Rom. 8:5-7).
3) They are to varying degrees necessary for life.
4) They are present, ever before us, and can be possessed right now.

b. Earthly riches are corruptible and destroyed (see DEEPER STUDY #1—Mt. 6:19). Something terrible happens to everything on earth. Everything ages, dies, deteriorates, and decays. Things are on the earth only for a brief time, and then they are no more. Everything has the seed of corruption and destruction within it.

c. Earthly riches are insecure. The things on earth are insecure for three reasons.
⇨ They can be stolen or eaten up.
⇨ They do not last; they waste away.
⇨ A person cannot take a single thing with him when he passes from this world.

For we brought nothing into the world, and we can take nothing out of it. (1 Tim. 6:7)

For the love of money is a root of all kinds of evil. Some people, eager for money, have wandered from the faith and pierced themselves with many griefs. (1 Tim. 6:10)

Your gold and silver are corroded. Their corrosion will testify against you and eat your flesh like fire. You have hoarded wealth in the last days. (James 5:3)

A flood will carry off his house, rushing waters on the day of God's wrath. (Job 20:28)

Man is a mere phantom as he goes to and fro: He bustles about, but only in vain; he heaps up wealth, not knowing who will get it. (Psa. 39:6)

For all can see that wise men die; the foolish and the senseless alike perish and leave their wealth to others. (Psa. 49:10)

Cast but a glance at riches, and they are gone, for they will surely sprout wings and fly off to the sky like an eagle. (Prov. 23:5)

For riches do not endure forever, and a crown is not secure for all generations. (Prov. 27:24)

I hated all the things I had toiled for under the sun, because I must leave them to the one who comes after me. (Eccl. 2:18)

Whoever loves money never has money enough; whoever loves wealth is never satisfied with his income. This too is meaningless. (Eccl. 5:10)

Like a partridge that hatches eggs it did not lay is the man who gains riches by unjust means. When his life is half gone, they will desert him, and in the end he will prove to be a fool. (Jer. 17:11)

By your wisdom and understanding you have gained wealth for yourself and amassed gold and silver in your treasuries. By your great skill in trading you have increased your wealth, and because of your wealth your heart has grown proud. (Ezek. 28:4-5)

Thought 1. Note four striking lessons.

1) Wealth is sought, and it is sought by many. What is often forgotten is this: every bit of wealth is held by someone. Therefore, many are always figuring how to get some of what someone else has. Things of the world are very insecure.

2) A man can be snatched away from this earth as quickly as the twinkling of an eye. Everything for which he has worked so hard on this earth can be gone immediately (cp. Lk. 12:16-21).

3) A man can lose much of what he has in this world and lose it quickly. He can lose it through financial difficulties, accident, marital problems, illness, death, and a myriad of other ways.

4) A person is a fool to seek an abundance of things—to grasp after more and more. Why? Because tonight or tomorrow or some day soon God will say, "You fool! This very night

your life will be demanded from you. Then who will get what you have prepared for yourself?" (Lk. 12:20). Christ says, "Anyone who stores up things for himself but is not rich toward God"—is going to hear the above (Lk. 12:21).

2. There are heavenly riches, There are things in heaven that believers desire. Christ calls these heavenly riches (see outline and notes—Eph.1:3 for the list of God's heavenly blessings). Heavenly riches would be such things as...
   • a blameless life
   • becoming a true child of God
   • the forgiveness of sins
   • wisdom
   • understanding the will of God (purpose, meaning, and significance in life)
   • an enormous inheritance that is eternal
   • a constant Comforter and Helper, the Holy Spirit of God Himself
   • life that is full, abundant, and overflowing (Jn. 10: 10)

Christ says three things about heavenly riches that are of critical importance to the believer and the unbeliever.

   a. Store up for yourselves heavenly riches. A person is foolish to seek and set his mind on perishable things. Why? Because he can seek after that which gives all the meaning, purpose, and significance to life that one can imagine. To have meaning and purpose and

significance in life is what life is all about.
Think about it. "A man's life does not consist
in the abundance of his possessions" (Lk.
12:15). How much meaning is there in
something that passes and perishes? Even
while a person seeks after something on this
earth, there is an inner awareness that it will
not last. There is an end to whatever meaning
he finds in it. The earthly treasure may be a
car, a job, a trip, a relationship, clothing,
position, power, fame, or fortune. The fact
is, no matter what the treasure is, it will end
and pass away and be no more. A worldly
man's meaning for living, his purpose and
significance in life, is temporary, unfulfilling
and incomplete. (See note 4 and DEEPER
STUDY #1—Eph. 1:7; note 5 and DEEPER
STUDY #1—2 Pet. 1:4; cp. Eph. 1:3.)

b. Heavenly riches are incorruptible. Corruption
can be escaped (2 Pet. 1:4). There is an
"inheritance that can never perish, spoil or
fade—kept in heaven for you" (1 Pet. 1:4).
Everyone should lay claim and set his heart
on *his* heavenly inheritance. Heavenly riches
are secure (see notes—Eph. 1:3). Thieves
cannot break through heaven; they cannot
penetrate the spiritual dimension. No one nor
anything can take away a person's heavenly
riches. The love of God assures this (cp. Rom.
8:32-39).

Thought 1. Christ does not stop a man from seeking treasure; contrariwise, He guides the man's search to real treasure. Heaven is worth more than all the wealth in the world. "What good will it be for a man if he gains the whole world, yet forfeits his soul? Or what can a man give in exchange for his soul?" (Mt. 16:26).

⇨ "What good is it for a man to gain the whole world, yet forfeit his soul?" (Mk. 8:36).

⇨ "What good is it for a man to gain the whole world, and yet lose or forfeit his very self?" (Lk. 9:25).

Thought 2. A man must leave all to follow Christ or else he cannot be the Lord's disciple.

In the same way, any of you who does not give up everything he has cannot be my disciple. (Luke 14:33)

Thought 3. Christ says a man is to store up treasures in heaven for himself, not store up treasures on earth for his family. A pointed and disturbing message to many!

But store up for yourselves treasures in heaven, where moth and rust do not destroy, and where thieves do not break in and steal. Jesus answered, (Mt. 6:20)

"If you want to be perfect, go, sell your possessions and give to the poor, and you will have treasure in heaven. Then come, follow me." (Mt. 19:21)

Sell your possessions and give to the poor. Provide purses for yourselves that will not wear out, a treasure in heaven that will not be exhausted, where no thief comes near and no moth destroys. (Luke 12:33)

What is more, I consider everything a loss compared to the surpassing greatness of knowing Christ Jesus my Lord, for whose sake I have lost all things. I consider them rubbish, that I may gain Christ (Phil. 3:8)

In this way they will lay up treasure for themselves as a firm foundation for the coming age, so that they may take hold of the life that is truly life. (1 Tim. 6:19)

I counsel you to buy from me gold refined in the fire, so you can become rich; and white clothes to wear, so you can cover your shameful nakedness; and salve to put on your eyes, so you can see. (Rev. 3:18)

DEEPER STUDY #1

(6:19) Perishable—Imperishable—Corruption—Incorruption: there is a seed of corruption and destruction within the world—a principle or nature of corruption and destruction within everything on earth. Everything is imperfectly born and formed; it ages, dies, deteriorates, decays, and wastes away. (See Deeper Study #2—Mt. 8:17; notes—1 Cor. 15:50; 2 Cor. 5:1-4; Col. 2:8; note 5 and Deeper Study #1— 2 Pet. 1:4.)

This was to fulfill what was spoken through the prophet Isaiah: "He took up our infirmities and carried our diseases." (Mt. 8:17)

I declare to you, brothers, that flesh and blood cannot inherit the kingdom of God, nor does the perishable inherit the imperishable. (1 Cor. 15:50)

Now we know that if the earthly tent we live in is destroyed, we have a building from God, an eternal house in heaven, not built by human hands....Because when we are clothed, we will not be found naked. (2 Cor. 5:1, 3)

Through these he has given us his very great and precious promises, so that through them you may participate in the divine nature and escape the corruption in the world caused by evil desires. (2 Pet. 1:4)

There is an imperishable, indestructible seed, a principle of incorruption, an eternal nature of incorruption in heaven (1 Pet. 1:4, 23; cp. 1:18-23; 2 Pet. 1:4; cp. 1 Cor. 15:12-58. See note—Eph. 1:3.)

Praise be to the God and Father of our Lord Jesus Christ! In his great mercy he has given us new birth into a living hope through the resurrection of Jesus Christ from the dead, and into an inheritance that can never perish, spoil or fade—kept in heaven for you. (1 Pet. 1:3-4)

For you have been born again, not of perishable seed, but of imperishable, through the living and enduring word of God. (1 Pet. 1:23)

So will it be with the resurrection of the dead. The body that is sown is perishable, it is raised imperishable; it is sown in dishonor, it is raised in glory; it is sown in weakness, it is raised in power; it is sown a natural body, it is raised a spiritual body. If there is a natural body, there is also a spiritual body. (1 Cor. 15:42-44; cp. 1 Cor. 15:12-58)

2 (6:21-23) ***Heart—Mind:*** Christ warns about two kinds of hearts.

1. There is the good heart. It is just like a good eye. Note that the eye is a gate that *gives entrance* to the mind of man. What man looks at is what he thinks about, and what he thinks about is what he actually becomes (cp. Pr. 23:7). If a man focuses upon Jesus Christ, who is the Light of the world (Jn. 8:12), then his mind and heart will be *full of light.* Therefore, the deeds of his body will be deeds of light. Singleness of the eye and heart means that a person sets his attention upon the Lord Jesus for the purpose of doing His will (cp. Acts 2:46; Eph. 6:5; Col. 3:22). An evil eye is one that focuses upon anything that is not of God.

A man's heart is precisely where his treasure is. If his treasure is on earth, his heart is on earth. If his treasure is in heaven, his heart is in heaven. The eye illustrates the truth. If a man's eye is *good and healthy,* then he is able to focus upon the treasure and grasp the truth. But if the eye is *unhealthy,* he is not able to focus upon the treasure. He is blind and in darkness. A *healthy heart* is like a healthy eye. It grasps the true treasure, the treasure in heaven. But an *unhealthy heart* is like an unhealthy eye. It is in darkness, unable to see the treasure in heaven.

Note that the believer fixes his eyes upon heaven for two primary reasons.

a. His citizenship is in heaven:

> *But our citizenship is in heaven. And we eagerly await a Savior from there, the Lord*

Jesus Christ, who, by the power that enables him to bring everything under his control, will transform our lowly bodies so that they will be like his glorious body. (Phil. 3:20-21)

b. He seeks the treasures which are eternal:

So we fix our eyes not on what is seen, but on what is unseen. For what is seen is temporary, but what is unseen is eternal. (2 Cor. 4:18)

⇨ They are indestructible (v. 20).
⇨ They are secure (v. 20).
⇨ They cause his whole body to be full of light (v. 22).
⇨ They consume his whole being in all the meaning and purpose and significance of life (v. 24).
⇨ They cause him to love and to serve God (v. 24).
⇨ They draw him near to God (v. 24).

When Jesus spoke again to the people, he said, "I am the light of the world. Whoever follows me will never walk in darkness, but will have the light of life." (John 8:12)

Before long, the world will not see me anymore, but you will see me. Because I live, you also will live. (John 14:19)

The man without the Spirit does not accept the things that come from the Spirit of God, for they are foolishness to him, and he cannot understand them, because they are spiritually discerned. (1 Cor. 2:14)

> *By faith he left Egypt, not fearing the king's anger; he persevered because he saw him who is invisible. (Heb. 11:27)*

Thought 1. The believer has a clear-cut charge: "Set your mind on things above, not on earthly things" (Col. 3:2).

Praise be to the God and Father of our Lord Jesus Christ, who has blessed us in the heavenly realms with every spiritual blessing in Christ. (Eph. 1:3)

I pray also that the eyes of your heart may be enlightened in order that you may know the hope to which he has called you, the riches of his glorious inheritance in the saints, (Eph. 1:18)

Although I am less than the least of all God's people, this grace was given me: to preach to the Gentiles the unsearchable riches of Christ, (Eph. 3:8)

He regarded disgrace for the sake of Christ as of greater value than the treasures of Egypt, because he was looking ahead to his reward. (Heb. 11:26)

Listen, my dear brothers: Has not God chosen those who are poor in the eyes of the world to be rich in faith and to inherit the kingdom he promised those who love him? (James 2:5)

2. There is the bad heart. It is just like a bad eye. A bad eye is not able to focus upon the treasure, not able to focus upon the things of God. A bad eye is blind and in darkness. So it is with the heart. Christ says that a person is not to set his heart upon earthly treasures. Why? Such a person

focuses his eyes (attention, mind, thoughts, energy, effort) on evil. What does Christ mean? Earthly things are evil because they are deceiving.

⇨ They are corruptible, perishable; they age, die, waste away, deteriorate, and decay.

⇨ They are insecure; they will be stolen or taken away or left behind.

⇨ They cause a person's heart to be full of darkness (v. 23).

⇨ They will consume a person (v. 24).

⇨ They cause a person to hate, despise, and reject God (v. 24).

⇨ They alienate a person from God (v. 24).

Thought 1. Several things happen to a man who sets his eye upon earthly things. The shadows of darkness set in upon him. He becomes deceived (cp. Mt. 13:7, 22). He is deceived in that he becomes...

• covetous and consuming (to get more and more).

• complaining and grudging.

• apprehensive and fearful (of losing it).

• hard and close-minded (to giving much). (Cp. Jas. 5:9.)

But if your eyes are bad, your whole body will be full of darkness. If then the light within you is darkness, how great is that darkness! (Mt. 6:23)

The light shines in the darkness, but the darkness has not understood it. (Jn. 1:5)

This is the verdict: Light has come into the world, but men loved darkness instead of light because their deeds were evil. (Jn. 3:19)

The god of this age has blinded the minds of unbelievers, so that they cannot see the light of the gospel of the glory of Christ, who is the image of God. (2 Cor. 4:4)

They are darkened in their understanding and separated from the life of God because of the ignorance that is in them due to the hardening of their hearts. (Eph. 4:18)

3 (6:24) **Decision:** Christ warns that a choice has to be made between two kinds of masters. There are two critical reasons why a choice has to be made.

1. A man hates one master and loves the other. When both masters call upon the man at the same time, he has to make a choice. He favors, serves, helps, and loves one; and while he is doing so, he is disfavoring, rejecting, and showing disrespect and hate for the other. A man cannot serve two masters.
2. A man either cleaves to or despises one of the masters. He has to choose which master to favor and serve. He has to cleave to one. In cleaving to one, he reveals disrespect and spite for the other. A man cannot serve two masters.

The choice is clear. A man either serves God or material things.

⇨ There are only two treasures: the earth and its treasures or God and His treasures, physical and material things or spiritual and eternal things.

⇨ Every man without exception has committed his life to one of two treasures: mammon or God. He is focusing his heart, eyes, mind, attention, thoughts, hands, and energy upon earthly things or upon heavenly things. He cannot "serve God <u>and money</u>. "

Thought 1. So many look at wealth as a blessing of God, a sign that one is godly. But the Bible says differently.

And constant friction between men of corrupt mind, who have been robbed of the truth and who think that godliness is a means to financial gain. But godliness with contentment is great gain. For we brought nothing into the world, and we can take nothing out of it. But if we have food and clothing, we will be content with that. People who want to get rich fall into temptation and a trap and into many foolish and harmful desires that plunge men into ruin and destruction. For the love of money is a root of all kinds of evil. Some people, eager for money, have wandered from the faith and pierced themselves with many griefs. But you, man of God, flee from all this, and pursue righteousness, godliness, faith, love, endurance and gentleness. (1 Tim. 6:5-11)

Thought 2. Money, earthly treasures, can be many things (see Mt. 6:19-20).

1) Riches and wealth.

   Now listen, you who say, "Today or tomorrow we will go to this or that city, spend a year there, carry on business and make money." (James 4:13)

   Now listen, you rich people, weep and wail because of the misery that is coming upon you. (James 5:1)

2) Food, the filling of one's stomach.

   Their destiny is destruction, their god is their stomach, and their glory is in their shame. Their mind is on earthly things. (Phil. 3:19)

3) An evil, lusting eye.

   But I tell you that anyone who looks at a woman lustfully has already committed adultery with her in his heart. (Mt. 5:28)

   But if your eyes are bad, your whole body will be full of darkness. If then the light within you is darkness, how great is that darkness! (Mt. 6:23)

   Greed, malice, deceit, lewdness, envy, slander, arrogance and folly. (Mark 7:22)

4) The craving of the sinful nature.

   Do not love the world or anything in the world. If anyone loves the world, the love of the Father is not in him. For everything in the world— the cravings of sinful man, the lust of his eyes and the boasting of what he has and does—

comes not from the Father but from the world.
(1 John 2:15-16)

5) Unproductive activity, relaxation, recreation, wasteful pastimes, sluggish feelings.

Go to the ant, you sluggard; consider its ways and be wise! It has no commander, overseer or ruler, yet it stores its provisions in summer and gathers its food at harvest. How long will you lie there, you sluggard? When will you get up from your sleep? A little sleep, a little slumber, a little folding of the hands to rest— and poverty will come on you like a bandit and scarcity like an armed man. (Prov. 6:6-11)

Thought 3. God promises several great things to the man who serves Him.

1) All the necessities of life.

But seek first his kingdom and his righteousness, and all these things will be given to you as well. (Mt. 6:33)

2) Freedom from anxiety.

Do not be anxious about anything, but in everything, by prayer and petition, with thanksgiving, present your requests to God. And the peace of God, which transcends all understanding, will guard your hearts and your minds in Christ Jesus. (Phil. 4:6-7)

3) Joy and contentment.

I have told you this so that my joy may be in you and that your joy may be complete. (John 15:11)

Keep your lives free from the love of money and be content with what you have, because God has said, "Never will I leave you; never will I forsake you." (Heb. 13:5)

4) Full, abundant, and eternal life.

"For God so loved the world that he gave his one and only Son, that whoever believes in him shall not perish but have eternal life. (John 3:16)

"I tell you the truth, whoever hears my word and believes him who sent me has eternal life and will not be condemned; he has crossed over from death to life. (John 5:24)

The thief comes only to steal and kill and destroy; I have come that they may have life, and have it to the full. (John 10:10)

DEEPER STUDY #2

(6:24) **Wealth:** see Deeper Study #1—
Mt. 19:16-22; notes—19:23-26; 19:27-30;
pt. 2 Jas. 1:9-11

• PURPOSE STATEMENT •

LEADERSHIP MINISTRIES WORLDWIDE

exists to equip ministers, teachers, and laymen
in·their understanding, preaching, and teaching of God's
Word by publishing and distributing worldwide
The Preacher's Outline & Sermon Bible®
and related ***Outline*** Bible materials, to reach &
disciple men, women, boys, and girls for Jesus Christ.

• MISSION STATEMENT •

1. To make the Bible so understandable - its truth so
   clear and plain - that men and women everywhere,
   whether teacher or student, preacher or hearer, can
   grasp its Message and receive Jesus Christ as Savior;
   and...

2. To place the Bible in the hands of all who will
   preach and teach God's Holy Word, verse by verse,
   precept by precept, regardless of the individual's
   ability to purchase it.

The ***Outline*** Bible materials have been given to LMW for
printing and especially distribution worldwide at/below
cost, by those who remain anonymous. One fact,
however, is as true today as it was in the time of Christ:

•The Gospel is free, but the cost of taking it is not•

LMW depends on the generous gifts of Believers with a
heart for Him and a love and burden for the lost. They
help pay for the translating, printing, and distributing of
Outline Bible materials in the hands of God's servants
worldwide who will present the Gospel message with
clarity, authority and understanding beyond their own.

LMW was incorporated in the state of Tennessee in July 1992 and received
IRS 501(c)(3) nonprofit status in March 1994. LMW is an international,
nondenominational mission organization. All proceeds from USA sales, along with
donations from donor partners, go 100% into underwriting our translation and
distribution projects of ***Outline*** Bible materials to preachers, church & lay
leaders, and Bible students around the world.